FAST WOMEN

PIONEERING AUSTRALIAN MOTORCYCLISTS

Pitstop is an imprint of Woodslane Press Pty Ltd
10 Apollo Street
Warriewood, NSW 2102
Email: info@woodslane.com.au
Tel: 02 8445 2300
www.woodslane.com.au
First published in Australia in 2017 by Woodslane Press
© 2017 Woodslane Press, text © 2017 Sally-Anne Fowles, images © as per photo credits

The information in this publication is based upon the current state of commercial and industry practice and the general circumstances as at the date of publication. Every effort has been made to obtain permissions relating to information reproduced in this publication. The publisher makes no representations as to the accuracy, reliability or completeness of the information contained in this publication. To the extent permitted by law, the publisher excludes all conditions, warranties and other obligations in relation to the supply of this publication and otherwise limits its liability to the recommended retail price. In no circumstances will the publisher be liable to any third party for any consequential loss or damage suffered by any person resulting in any way from the use or reliance on this publication or any part of it. Any opinions and advice contained in the publication are offered solely in pursuance of the author's and publisher's intention to provide information, and have not been specifically sought.

National Library of Australia Cataloguing-in-Publication entry

Creator:	Fowles, Sally-Anne, author.
Title:	Fast women : pioneering Australian motorcyclists / Sally-Anne Fowles.
ISBN:	9781925403725 (paperback)
Subjects:	Fowles, Sally-Anne.
	Motorcyclists--Australia--Biography.
	Motorcyclists--Australia--Anecdotes.
	Motorsports--Australia--History.

Printed in China via Asia Pacific
Cover image: Kim Krebs, photo by Dominik Siedlecki
Page iii image: Sydney Women's Motorcycle Club (courtesy Monica Stewart and Margaret Williams)
Book design by: Jenny Cowan

FAST WOMEN

PIONEERING AUSTRALIAN MOTORCYCLISTS

ACKNOWLEDGMENTS

With thanks to all who have helped in the creation of this book.

My wonderfully supportive family: Ian Fowles, Frank (Dad) and Margaret (Mum) Wilson, Nicole, Mark and Samuel Cook, Carlee & Tyson, Lauren & Mark, Elle & Madison and Carolyn Bennett.

Also: Judi Denton, Corinna Steeb & Frank Sampson, Carolyn Lewis, Dale Rutledge, Robin Lewis, Jim Scaysbrook, Cynthia Atkin, Yvonne Barker, Wes Brown, George Bolton, Paul Carter, Heather Ellis, Suzie Q, Jan & Phil, Geoff Groth, Natalie Lambourn, Mike & Shannon at Reid Print, Michael Mahar, Ian McDonald, Bill Runciman, Jo Runciman, Josh Walker, Margaret Williams, Eric Williams, Darryl Woodhouse, Judith Zielinski.

Sponsors: The District Council of Mount Barker (South Australia), The Prancing Pony Brewery and Girl Rider Pty Ltd.

CONTENTS

FOREWORD

To a motorcyclist, the reason we ride needs no explanation, but for those unfamiliar with the joy and sense of freedom it brings, it can only be described as an unparalleled experience of simultaneous exhilaration and peace. Exhilaration through the adrenalin hit we get from the sensation of flying through the air, unimpeded by a steel cage, with the wind passing over you and the roar of the engine in your ears. And peace, as you exist totally in the moment, undistracted, focused only on carving the corner ahead or just relaxing and taking in the scenery and scents.

With so much to offer, this sport, this activity, this passion, is increasingly being enjoyed by girls and women along with boys and men. Participating in competition, supporting the sport through journalism, running club events, or simply getting on a bike to ride recreationally no longer raises eyebrows. The women in this book are the reason why. They have pioneered the way forward and are the reason we now see more women realising the opportunities, friendships and passion that comes from being on two wheels.

I wish I had had this book when I was a little girl. Every page inspires courage, determination, individualism and achievement. No matter what your aspirations as a motorcyclist, these stories will help you realise your own riding dream and, if not already, will see you appreciate motorcycling in a whole new light.

Tania Lawrence
FIM Oceania and Motorcycling Australia President 2015–16

INTRODUCTION

"Twenty years from now you will be more disappointed by the things you didn't do than by the ones you did do.
So, throw off the bowlines. Sail away from the safe harbor.
Catch the trade winds in your sails.
Explore. Dream. Discover."

Mark Twain

I was raised on a rural property in between Forbes and West Wyalong in NSW, which is where I had my first relationship with a motorcycle. The Yamaha Agricultural 'Ag' bike was a crucial work horse to Dad and Mum, transporting them around our 3000-acre property and used for rounding up the cattle and sheep, with our working dog 'Jack' always perched on the back. This bike was more than just a source of fun for me, it delivered the exhilaration of simply being myself and being within myself as I zoomed across the dusty paddocks, racing the grain trains that thundered past.

As for many country kids, the bright lights of city life beckoned and I headed off for Sydney at the age of 18, so beginning a 20-year hiatus from being aboard a bike. My weekly 'fix' was my pilgrimage to the Harley Davidson dealership in Chatswood every weekend. I was 19 when my ultimate vision of motorcycle perfection, the Harley Davidson 'Fat Boy', was released. Armed with the marketing brochure and a genuine pair of Harley Davidson boots, but not with financial savvy, the dream slipped away from me, however it was clearly imprinted firmly in the recesses of my subconscious.

Fortune found me when I met my wonderful husband, Ian, whose life-long passion and exuberance for motorcycles reignited the flame that resided in me. With Ian's encouragement and support and Mark Twain's inspirational quote singing in my ears, at the ripe age of 38, I gained my road licence, and so followed the exhilarating and challenging journey of learning that lead to owning my dream Harley Davidson Fat Boy.

In 2013, as my passion grew, I went searching for stories about like-minded women that I could relate to and women who had previously discovered the joy of motorcycling. I soon came to realise these stories were hard to find. Where could I find the literature that presented Australian women's stories that I craved to read? As any avid motorcyclist understands, a journey to a newsagent or bookstore is a constant search for writing that satisfies the rider's soul. After placing a very simple advertisement in the free, 'Can you help?' section of the Adelaide *Advertiser* 'Sunday Mail', I was inundated with phone calls and emails from women and men who expressed heartfelt stories of themselves, their mothers, aunts and sisters, aboard their two-wheeled steeds. Every story, every expression and every photo received, told me that I was on the tip of a very inspiring and historically significant 'iceberg'.

My only recollection of History class during my high school years, yes, relayed facts from ancient Greece to World War II. But for me, and I would imagine for many students, it didn't feel real. In my teenaged brain, there was no link to the fact that my predecessors were no different in anatomy to me, had the same life concerns – making a crust, paying the bills and raising children and pursued their enjoyment and passion wherever it laid. But these incredible women's stories that poured in from my advertisement struck a chord.

The importance of telling these stories now really hit home while caring for our 2½ year old granddaughter, who was playing with two toy motorbikes, I said to her *"Are they your motorbikes?"* and she said matter of factly, *"No Nanny, girls don't have motorbikes!"*

Had someone told her this or was it simply that she had only observed little boys on their Pee Wee 50s in rural South Australia? In this same week my beloved father had turned 80! Many of the women featured in the book, owned and relished their motorcycles many years before my father was even born. Thankfully for my beautiful granddaughters, the world is now more open for them to live their dreams and to explore, dream and discover.

So, with that, I am extremely grateful and humble that I have the opportunity to present *'FAST WOMEN – pioneering Australian motorcyclists'.*

Sally-Anne Fowles

1
MISS JANE QUEAIN
AUSTRALIAN TRAILBLAZER

Miss Jane Queain was most certainly an extraordinary woman. Although little is known about her life, she is considered one of the earliest pioneering female motorcyclists in Australia and it is understood that she was the first lady in South Australia to ride her own machine.

Miss Queain grew up in Minlaton on the Yorke Peninsula of South Australia, approximately 125 miles (202 km) to the west of Adelaide. In the early 1900s Minlaton was considered remote from the capital city Adelaide, as horse-powered vehicles were mainly of the four-legged variety.

Jane was a well known teacher of music and art and her dedication saw her driving her pair of ponies in a loop of approximately 150 km over rocky, unsealed, challenging roads to regularly reach her students. Finding that she lost considerable time travelling these distances, in April of 1913 she decided to purchase a motorcycle, a 2¾ (horsepower) Douglas. The fact that Miss Queain was able to acquire her Douglas, considering she resided on the other side of the globe from her acquisition, was quite astounding as motorcycles with internal combustion engines were only made commercially available in Europe in the late 1880s and it was at a time when product marketing was minimal and freight services were slow.

Capturing more than just a moment in history, the only known photograph of Miss Queain reflects the style of the era. Wearing pants or even skirts above the ankle was certainly not considered appropriate attire for a woman in the early 20th century, so Jane wore her full length silk skirts and gowns on her teaching rounds and only her large leather gauntlet gloves for protection. As for comfort, her Douglas motorcycle was in-itself a challenge! With only a minimal bicycle-type seat, springer front end and no rear shocks it certainly would not have been the most hospitable form of transport on the rough, unsealed roads of country South Australia. But

Jane loved it and her first feelings of nervousness soon wore off!

"Now I don't seem to be able to travel fast enough" she declared.

"I've had one or two falls, but that's all in the game. Once the skirt of my silk dustcoat became caught in the flywheel, and then I nearly went. I managed to pull up in time, however, and released it. On several occasions I've run over snakes, but they were only small ones. All the girls on the Peninsula are in love with my Douglas, and I think that very soon many others will get motor cycles. I save quite two-thirds of my time now, and not only is the machine quicker than ponies, but it is also more convenient. There is nothing to compare with motor cycling, and I'm sorry for those poor people who cannot indulge in it. It is wonderfully exhilarating, and it is impossible to describe the glorious sensation that one gets when travelling on a speedy machine. I'm glad I've got a motor cycle and I don't think I'll ever give it up"' (The Register, 22 October 1913).

Miss Jane Queain's desire for adventure took her from Minlaton to Paris in 1914 to study art and it is believed that she returned to Australia to teach art at Loreto Catholic School for Girls in Kirribilli, Sydney.

To date, Miss Jane Queain's life story is a mystery and who knows if her desire for motorcycling continued?

Photo supplied by Mr Michael Mahar (great-nephew)

2

EVELYN 'BOBBIE' ROBERTS

A GYPSY AT HEART

At 3 am, the depths of the dark, foggy extreme early hours of the morning did not bother avid and courageous motorcyclist Miss Evelyn 'Bobbie' Roberts. She was competing in a Midnight trial hosted by her beloved Indian Motorcycle Club of Victoria. This was only one of the events held annually for their dedicated club members and it was not for the fainthearted. Setting off on a reliability trial departing at midnight, with no street lights, no sealed roads and on the undulating hills of the Dandenong Ranges, 'Bobbie' missed the road between Monbulk and Lilydale, and to make matters worse, she ran out of fuel. She was not able to progress until the morning light's first passer-by topped her up. There was no doubt in the minds of the rest of the club that Miss Roberts would finish the trial, she was an accomplished rider and they knew that

1928   PAGE FIFTEEN

SCORNED THE WEATHER during the Indian motor cyclists' tour from Melbourne to Sydney last week.—Miss R. E. Roberts, of Kyneton, the only woman to ride a solo machine of the party of 108. She wore riding breeches and oilskins.

Evelyn featured in The Sun newspaper, Melbourne.

1927 - Victoria's Indian Motorcycle Club, Gypsy tour photographed in the main street of Bairnsdale Victorian. Can you spot Evelyn? Photograph courtesy Darryl Woodhouse.

OFF ON A LONG TREK went members of the Indian Club, on Saturday. They will travel 1300 miles on a tour to Sydney.—Miss E. Roberts, the only girl rider, ready to leave.

Evelyn noted "as the only female rider": in The Sun *newspaper, Melbourne.*

she could attend to any mechanical challenges her mount threw at her.

The progressive club attracted many participants to their inaugural Gypsy Tour of 1926, with the itinerary boldly taking the riders from Melbourne to Adelaide and back. The following year's Gypsy Tour of 1927 was their

1928 – Victoria's Indian Motorcycle Club, Gypsy tour photographed outside Absolom's Motor Garage in Launceston, Tasmania. Photograph courtesy Darryl Woodhouse.

most celebrated and reported tour in the media. Forty Indian machines and their riders departed Melbourne on Christmas Eve, riding 1500 miles (2414 kilometres) along the coastline to Sydney and they were only allowed three days and nights on the run over and five nights on the return journey.

Evelyn, described as the 'plucky Richmond girl', was the only female rider on the tour. Riding her beloved Indian Prince and with her never-failing spirit, 'Bobbie' relished the challenges of trial riding. As reported by Motorcycle Sparkings – The Truth 17-12-1927 she *"has once again proved that she is no mean hand as a motorcyclist. She is mounted on a solo Indian Prince, has actually shown some of the male members of the club a few points on the art of driving'. Coming down twice while her Indian Prince was negotiating the long run stretch reportedly made no difference to her geniality. Upon arriving in Sydney more than 100 Sydney Indian club riders met the Victorians at Tom Ugly's point."*

Every day of the club's Gypsy Tours was full to the brim of riding and revelry. There was great camaraderie amongst the clan of riders and,at the conclusion of the day's long ride, they were hosted to gala dinners and concerts by Indian Club members of the towns they passed through. Upon their arrival into Sydney, they were treated to a moonlight harbour trip where it was reported that *"Those appearing the freshest at the conclusion were the girl rider, Miss. R. Roberts, and Matt Attwater"* (unknown newspaper article). Matt Attwater, one of the club's characters, was known as the camp alarm clock, rousing the

Evelyn aboard her Indian Prince, in an unknown newspaper article.

other sleeping club members bright and early with his antics. There was also livewire 'Dad' Brookshaw (with his wife precariously seated in sidecar) who became bitten by the speed bug overtaking the main bunch riding alongside the Sydney express for about two miles, and prankster and cork artist Joe Molloy who blackened the faces of his sleeping companions with burnt cork, whilst camping out at the Sydney showground. Alas, got his just desserts when a good dose of castor oil was poured down poor sleeping Joe's neck.

In the early months of 1928 excitement grew in Tasmania as the acclaimed and much publicised Indian Gypsy Tour had been enticed by the Launceston chapter of the Indian Motorcycle club to book its Christmas event on the island in July of 1928. The ten-day trip took in the sights of Cataract Gorge, Burnie, Deloraine, Wynyard, Beaconsfield, St Columba Falls, St Helens, Hobart and the Great Lake.

Miss Evelyn 'Bobbie' Roberts featured front and centre of the grand group photograph concluding what is believed to be the final Gypsy Tour held by the Victorian Indian Motorcycle club of the 1920s.

Photos supplied by Mr Darryl Woodhouse

3

THE NATIONAL EMERGENCY SERVICES WOMEN'S MOTORCYCLE MESSENGER CORPS – WORLD WAR II

At the beginning of World War II, the call of duty sat firmly in the minds of Australian civilians, determined to assist in any way possible to support their country at war.

When an advertisement in the *Sydney Morning Herald* (1940) called for women to join the National Emergency Services, the spark of ignition in the minds of these women excited a nation.

The National Emergency Services (NES) of New South Wales was established in 1939 to help protect, educate and provide aid on the home front. Civilians volunteered their time and services, akin to 'The Home Guard' in England.

Women in most Australian capital cities formed voluntary motorcycle despatch units, which provided Australia with a 'silent service', even though media interest was intense. Women riders were glamorised, and idolised in the media, reflecting the desire of the Australian leaders to keep up the morale of Australian society.

The need for secrecy was firmly understood by the Women of Despatch, who delivered crucial messages and provided an efficient link between wardens, camp barracks, ambulances, and hospitals, when "on air" methods of communications were not advised or if a crisis occurred that rendered normal methods of communications out of action.

The women's auxiliary of the Central Motorcycle Club (Sydney, NSW) was a driving force behind the formation of the NES Women's Motorcycle Messenger Corps. Businessman Mr. M.J. Doogan, attempted to inspire many organisations to form this service. However, most were stretched at the time by the enormity of the requirement for war time assistance. Many of the women were taught to ride by Doogan, but for business reasons he was unable to continue the training after a few months. Due to the efforts of Miss Anne McLaughlan and Mrs Margaret Golder, the Corps were able to continue. Realising the importance of the despatch service, Miss A. McLaughlan, a foundation member of the National Emergency Services ambulance drivers, volunteered her time and skills, undertaking the task of recruiting, and organising the training programme for the women.

Recruiting advertisements in newspapers were easily filled, with many women who were already keen motorcyclists (some belonging to the Sydney Women's Motorcycle club, see Chapter 5), answering the call.

Riding training took place at Centennial Park, Sydney, where women who did not own their own motorcycle trained on a Royal Enfield 2 stroke and were versed in tight manoeuvres, mechanics, first aid and stretcher drills.

As reported in the *Sydney Morning Herald* on 13 August 1940

'NEW WAR UNIT.

Item of the proposed training scheme for the National Emergency Services Women's Motor Cycle Messenger Corps, of which the first annual general meeting took place at 149 Castlereagh Street last night. Motor Cycle riding and maintenance, first aid, physical training, signalling, and squad field drill will also be included in the programme.

The organisation hopes to provide communication between wardens, ambulances, hospitals, and similar bodies if a disruption of normal communications occurred. Several women motor cyclists were among those present. Miss Eve Warnaby, of Liverpool has been a motor cyclist for eight years, and travelled to town on her machine, returning with Miss Nancy Russell as pillion rider. Miss Warnaby has motor cycled to Adelaide and back.

Miss D. Bray was elected president, Misses A. McLaughlan and Simpson vice-presidents, Mrs V. Golder honorary secretary, Miss J. Blanchfield honorary assistance secretary, and Miss B. Hanken honorary treasurer. Mr M.J. Doogan presided last night.'

Many of the women were already skilled at competition scrambling, road racing and hill climbs. In 1940, women were not permitted to compete in organised, licenced club rides/ races so they formed their own clubs, which in turn gave them the skill and determination to ride their own motorcycles for the service of their country.

The beauty of this tale is that the Women of the National Emergency Services Women's Motor Cycle Messenger Corps volunteered their own time, paid for their own uniforms and most supplied their own motorcycles.

'Cost of each item of uniform is: Cap, 6s 11d; gloves, 16s 11d; goggles 2s; NES badge, 1s 6d; arm badges, 2s; coat, £3; breeches, £1 15s; boots, £1 15s. Each member pays for own uniform, which was smartly tailored and dark blue in colour.' PIX Magazine 1942 (s = shillings, d = penny, £ = Pound).

As the sun set and the shroud of darkness descended, headlights were not allowed on despatch deliveries. So, riders were trained to ride, despatch messages and

Nancy Campbell and unknown in uniform.

*Miss Shirley Winter, Left, and Miss Eve Warnaby, women motorcycle messengers of the National Emergency Service, riding their Royal Enfield and Velocette machines through the city. Image is owned by **Australian War Memorial (image reference: 006678)**.*

repair their motorcycles even in the depths of the night. On their watch, they slept beside their motorcycles at the ready for their purpose.

On the 9th day of the 12th month 1941, one rider (un-named) despatched the following telegrams:

From the Prime Minister of Australia John Curtin to the State Premiers:

'Following Telegram has been received from Secretary of State for dominion affairs dated London 8th December 1941 2.26 pm begins His Majesty's Ambassador at Tokyo has been instructed to make the following communication at once to the Japanese Govt. Paragraph. On the evening of December 7th His Majesty's Govt in the United Kingdom learnt that Japanese forces without previous warning either in the form of a Declaration of War or of an ultimatum with a conditional declaration of War had attempted a landing on the coast of Malaya and bombed Singapore and Hong Kong. Paragraph. In view of these wanton acts of unprovoked aggression committed in flagrant violation of International Law and particularly of Article 1 of the third Hague Convention relative to the opening of hostilities to which both Japan and the United Kingdom are parties I have the honour to inform the Imperial Japanese Govt. in the name of His Majesty's Govt. of the United Kingdom that a State of War exists between the two countries. Ends.

And from the Governor General to the subjects of Australia:

Commonwealth of Australia Gazette issued today contains the following Proclamation. Begins.

I Alexander Gore Arkwright Baron Gowrie The Governor General aforesaid acting with the advice of the Federal Executive Council and in the exercise of all powers me thereunto enabling do hereby declare and proclaim that a State of War with the Japanese Empire exists and has existed in the Commonwealth of Australia and it's Territories as from the Eight Day of December One Thousand Nine Hundred and Forty One at Five O'clock in the afternoon reckoned according to the Standard Time in the Australian Capital Territory Colony of all which his Majesty's Loving Subjects and all others whom these presents may concern are hereby required to take notice and to govern themselves accordingly.

(Note: Brigadier General Alexander Gore Arkwright (Hore-Ruthven, 1st Earl of Gowrie) was a British soldier and Colonial Governor and the tenth Governor General of Australia).

The weight of these announcements never diminished the women's spirits in service to Australia.

Some Members of The National Emergency Services Women's Motorcycle Messenger Corps were:

Miss Eve Warnaby was the only woman to be permanently attached (on a voluntary basis) to the Recruiting Hut, Martin Place, Sydney. Prior to her Despatch days, Eve had ridden her own motorcycle for 8 years, purchasing her Velocette motorcycle in mid 1935. By the time, she was riding Despatch (riding an Ariel), she had owned five machines and covered approximately 40,000 miles (approximately 64,373 km). Enjoying social runs with the AJS Motorcycle club, Eve rode solo to Adelaide and back and enjoyed the thrill of the Grand Prix race events at Bathurst. Miss Warnaby also provided a valued service within country NSW. When a country doctor was urgently needed, a message carried on her motorcycle brought medical aid quickly. With many miles under her belt in rural areas, she was a experienced rider, who had the skill to take a bush track where even a car could not travel.

Mrs Margaret Golder (Deputy Chief) understood the complexities of the task, including performing mechanical repairs. She certainly championed the cause and not only instructed the women in riding skills, but also trained the women in mental fortitude, if, for example, they were intercepted in the dead of night on crucial deliveries. Her husband, Vince Golder, also performed NES despatch services and was Club Captain of the Sydney Central Motorcycle Club.

Mrs Hazel Mayes' (nee Flick) personal life was immersed in motorcycling from a very young age when her father would take her to motorcycle races and the Speedway. Hazel joined the Motorcycle Corps after seeing the advertisement in the *Sydney Morning Herald*. She was hooked, even going without lipstick and walking sections of the tram-ride home, just so she could save for her very own BSA (a 1937 250cc BSA). Hazel went on to enlist with the Air Force and trained as a flight mechanic, earning the position as a member of the Women's Auxiliary Australian Air Force (stationed in Wagga, NSW), stripping down, servicing and re-assembling twin-engine Beau fighters (strike craft used in the Pacific). Post war, Hazel returned to Sydney working as a Despatch rider for Kodak, *"I had pulled up in George Street one day beside a tram, a fellow lent out of the tram and yelled "Why don't you give a man back his job?" So, I went back to Riley Street and resigned"* (Interview of Hazel Mayes in *'Highside'* by Bruce Williams and Reece Scannell). This comment devastated Hazel and later in life she still relayed how much it hurt. Hazel's life remained involved in motorcycling with her husband, Bill, she participated in disciplines such as dirt track speedway races and club sporting trials, hill climbs and more. They were fervent members of the Central Motorcycle Club and Hazel was also a member of The Sydney Women's Motorcycle Club and a member of The Women's International Motorcycling Association. Hazel and Bill kept up intense involvement in the sport until 1956 when Bill was killed during the Ampol around Australia Road Trial.

Nancy Campbell in action.

Hazel raised their three children, worked in the motorcycle shop that her husband ran with other partners, then went on to work for Victa. Hazel Mayes passed away 2015 – Vale.

Miss Nancy Campbell was also a member of the Sydney Women's Motorcycle Club. Nancy enjoyed riding with her sisters, Margaret (Midge) and Monica. The three sisters were a driving force behind the inception of the Club. In the 1930s/40s it was forbidden for women to compete in registered Motorcycle race events. Not deterred, Nancy and her sisters created a club where women had the opportunity to enjoy the excitement of competing against each other in all types of disciplines. As a 24-year-old, Nancy's determination and dedication to ride wasn't quashed even after a major accident when her motorcycle skidded across Gladesville Bridge in Sydney. Nancy's pillion passenger 16-year-old, Elma Flick (Hazel Mayes' sister), was pinned under the bike but managed to scramble out. Nancy's skull was severely fractured and she was not expected to live but she survived and continued her love affair with motorcycles and became a valued and valuable National Emergency Services Despatch rider.

Miss Lurline Horsley, an 18-year-old shop assistant at David Jones and competition figure Roller Skater, was described in a *PIX* Magazine article from 1942 as "an all-round sports girl and a typical NES Despatch woman, skilled in many arts and also mastering the art of motorcycling".

In February 1942 there were 16 licenced women despatch riders and nine in training for the important and heralded position. The smartly tailored Women of Despatch always cut fine figures through the melancholy in war time cities. Sentinels of deliverance in stylish attire, they provided a glimmer of hope and order amid the uncertainty and despair of a war that only seemed to grow in intensity.

One rider had the honour and jubilance of despatching the telegram that brought the news of surrender and the end of the horrors of World War II.

Photos pg 17 and 21 supplied by Margaret Williams

Photo pg 18 from the Australian War Memorial

4

JUNE PARKER

AN ADVENTUROUS AND CHARITABLE SPIRIT

In 1941, at 15 years of age June Parker was already engaging and unconventional. Her entry into society did not involve debutante dresses and society balls. Even from an early age June was an enthralling and believable storyteller, only lying about her age so as to join the Australian Women's Land Army (AWLA). She did this not for rebellion or attention seeking, but only in an attempt to assist her country and the war effort.

World War II pressed on, and labour shortages within the farming sector of Australia instigated the formation of the AWLA. June accompanied many other Auxiliary members who were employed to perform such duties as fruit and vegetable production, and animal husbandry. To be eligible to enlist, women had to be between the ages of 18 and 50 and be British subjects or immigrants from Allied nations. The majority of women originated from city areas as they were not eligible to enlist if they were already a farmer, a rural employee, or a relative of a land holder.

Her father, Councillor and Mayor of Ringwood, Victoria, H.E. Parker, was a great inspiration, encouraging her to live her dreams and follow her heart. June was born into a maternal line of intuitives, and raised by women whose passionate beliefs were spiritualism, metaphysics, tarot cards and clairvoyance. Her grandmother was always taking in the homeless and mothers and babies who had nowhere to go. So June's psyche was ingrained with compassion, empathy and the importance of helping others in need.

June and Pat on the verge of their journey, loading up with raffle tickets.

June fell in love with the rural lifestyle she experienced whilst with the AWLA, and after the war decided to stick to outdoor life. She lived on a cattle station, and took up smoking so that she would be entitled to take a 'smoko' with the boys, and developed an ambition not only to bring cattle from the Northern Territory to Adelaide, but also to own her own sheep station.

However, at 21, June's immediate dream was to ride and explore Australia on a motorcycle. So that is what she did!

June purchased her motorcycle when her father refused her the use of the family car and she wanted to be independent. With only one hour's teaching before obtaining her licence, she clocked 4000 miles within a year on her BSA, and even though June had four brothers and two sisters, they *never* borrowed her motorcycle.

June was the embodiment of the determination of young women who graciously and eagerly filled the shoes of the men who had been sent to war. It was a time of great realisation where women who had formerly sat in the culturally-expected background rose to many occasions.

After the war, June's spirit of adventure guided her to advertise for a female motorcycle riding companion to tour and explore Victoria. Her charitable spirit inspired her concept of raising funds for the Returned Services League (RSL) whilst on tour. Patriotic work was nothing new to June as she had been involved in voluntary Red Cross work for some years.

June Parker had the 'gift of the gab' and had *"an amazing knack of engaging people and getting them swept up in whatever was interesting her at the time."* (*A Life Fully Lived* by Lesley Antonoff)

Miss Pat Hansford (21) was the selected woman who answered June's call and she became June's travelling companion, riding her own motorcycle. Pat was accomplished in her own right. She spent the wartime years with the Department of Aircraft Production, where she introduced a device which doubled the output of a duplicating machine. Pat was inspired and determined to become an authoress and had previously written children's stories which were published in Australian and American magazines and papers.

So, June and Pat set off from Elizabeth Street, Melbourne on their charitable tour of Victoria, raising funds

June's love of motorcycles is evident here whilst experiencing a race meet.

for the Middle Park RSL, in aid of its Memorial Hall and Free Kindergarten Building Fund. Handsome prizes in the Building Fund Appeal included a modern home valued at £4,000, a Dodge sedan and luxury caravan and a Dodge utility.

June rode a BSA 250 and Pat a BSA 125. The women were very proud of their motorcycles reporting that they had had no trouble with the machines since they started their journey. Their only disappointment was on arrival in Cobram – their bikes were not as *"spick and span"* as they had been earlier on their journey, but that was due to heavy rain and bad roads. When they departed Cobram their machines were as bright as pins. It is reported that the BSA 250 motorcycle was Australian built and was being tested in general running. It is unknown how June acquired the BSA (Australian produced) test bike and the history or outcome of the test bike is to date unknown.

"Women need not be out of any fun in motorcycle clubs if they ride their own machines. Formerly they stayed behind and merely acted in their social sphere. There is nothing wrong with women riding motorcycles provided they do not get machines which are too heavy for them to handle. There is no difference between a woman riding a motorcycle and a pedal bicycle. Women have more sense than the boys, and are not inclined to show off like the men do. Women generally are also more considerate to other people, and that applies to the road as well". (June Parker – unknown newspaper interview April 1949)

Every town brought an entirely new experience.

Arriving in Rochester (near Echuca), Victoria, well after midnight, they had no place to camp. June and Pat found the Rochester showgrounds and set up camp under a large pepper tree near the pavilions and sale yards. Waking up to bright sunshine several hours later, they were rather startled to find themselves surrounded by a crowd of people, in the midst of a pig sale. June and Pat hurriedly adjourned to a less crowded area, followed by the curious glances of the auctioneers and farmers.

Unfortunately, their opinion of Echuca as a nice town was considerably lowered following the theft of a number of articles from their motorcycles, which were parked outside the local Astoria Café. Their kit, including promotions flags and pennants and their riding goggles was stolen by lowly thieves while June and Pat were having supper.

Even after these events, the two determined women were not daunted and carried on.

"People are wonderful. Anyone else with a motorbike will always stop and do anything to help you. We have met a lot of nice people and are looking forward to meeting more".

Later in life June relayed to her daughter, Lesley, that when she wanted men to buy tickets from her she would ensure she was always sitting down and would look up slowly at them through her eyelashes. She said, *"they always bought more that way!"* June was the ultimate sales-lady without compromising her integrity!

Sleeping under haystacks, in stables, and a disused bake house shared with a horse for company, the two women generally *"roughed it"*, but both regarded it as *"good fun"*. *"One evening they could not find somewhere to sleep and decided to spend the night in an abandoned barn. They awoke in a panic to the sound of heavy breathing just outside their window. They lay awake all night clutching each other and as dawn broke they peeped out to find they were surrounded by a herd of cows".* (*A Life Fully Lived* by Lesley Antonoff)

Sketchy details in newspapers reported that Pat Hansford was injured in a car collision in July of 1949. Battered and bruised she was laid up in hospital for one month. Due to the mishap, Pat was unfortunately compelled to withdraw from the tour.

June continued on alone, successfully completing the fund-raising tour and satisfying the dream she had originally envisaged.

In November 1949, the BSA 250 test bike was returned and June's next pride and joy came in the form of a Triumph Tiger 100.

June had earned her stripes! Her months of charitable touring earned her the respect of the most revered names in Australian motorcycling of the time. Applauded and invited, June attended Scrambling at Castlemaine Vic., Road racing at Ballarat and Flinders Naval Base Vic., Mud battling at Gladstone Park Vic., Grass track racing at Warragul, and Airstrip racing at Valleyfield Tas. Her and her club comrades' bikes were nervously hoisted in

June and Part leaving Elizabeth Street, Melbourne 1949.

June, comfortable on her motorcycle.

nets onto the ferry to Tasmania to attend the Valleyfield races. Faces at the race included legendary Australian racers such as Ken Kavanagh and Ray Owens.

Hugh Antonoff unexpectedly came into June's life when on a slippery road she lost control and crashed her Triumph Tiger. Dragging it to a nearby location, she apparently "threw it" at a man who was innocently standing by, saying *"mind my bike, I'm late for work, I'll come back and get it later."* She said *"I kind of liked him and we just stuck together from that point on".*

June's adventures with motorcycling were realised.

"It's the open spaces, they're beaut. And there's a special clan among motorcyclists. They all want to help me." June Antonoff (nee Parker). Adventuress. Vale – 2006.

Photos supplied by – Mr Hugh Antonoff and Mr Ian McDonald

*Sky-larking with the group.
Margaret "Midge" Donkin
on right at top holding the
other lady.*

5

THE THREE SISTERS

and THE SYDNEY WOMEN'S MOTOR CYCLE CLUB

Avid motorcyclists, determined not to miss out on the challenge of competition, the three sisters Margaret, Monica and Nancy Donkin were crucial in the formation of the Sydney Women's Motorcycle Club. Many of the members of the club were also associated with the Central Motor Cycle Club of Sydney to which their husbands belonged. The Central MCC's members had the opportunity to compete in registered race events Australia-wide, including the 1954 Redex Reliability Trial (Monica's husband Keith being the outright winner), the Bathurst Grand Prix and Ballarat Grand Prix events. However, in 1948, women competing in events were strictly restricted to in-club reliability trials. Road racing was forbidden and, even in group recreational rides, the women were resigned to riding behind the men. Many were experienced riders that rode many miles interstate to watch their husbands and other Central members compete in Grand Prix events.

Young, brave and daring, Margaret, Monica and Nancy, along with their friends, did not submit to rules and regulations and both defiantly and joyously created The Sydney Women's Motorcycle Club so that they could experience the exhilaration of competition and racing.

And so follows a beautiful, visual portrayal of the three sisters Margaret, Monica and Nancy Donkin and their friends who shared in their passion for motorcycling.

Monica Stewart (nee Donkin) riding her sister Nancy's motorcycle.

Photos supplied by – Margaret Williams (nee Donkin) and Monica Stewart (nee Donkin).

Below: Nancy Campbell (nee Donkin) riding the bike she rode for the National Emergency Service Despatch Corps, note the blackout blades on the headlight.

Above: The Sydney Women's Motorcycle club in uniform, ready to ride.

Right: Margaret "Midge" Donkin racing against fellow club member only known as "Butch" with Mrs. Margaret Golder (Deputy-Chief N.E.S Motorcycle Despatch Corps- see chapter 3) waiving white flag.

Margaret "Midge" Donkin, aged 16/17, riding ring return event with other club members at back.

Margaret "Midge" Donkin posing for The Sun *Newspaper. To date she doesn't know why the journalist asked her to knit. She had never knitted a stitch in her life.*

Winifred sets off from Perth.

6
WINIFRED WELLS
THE HEROINE OF AN UNIMAGINABLE EPIC RIDE

CHAPTER 6

"Travellers on the long overland route across Australia were amazed to see a girl, travelling alone on a high-powered motor cycle, flash past them with a cheery wave. The lone rider was Winifred Wells, of Derby Road, Shinton Park, spending three weeks holiday by travelling 5505 miles from her home city of Perth to Sydney and back." (*People* Magazine, April 11,1951)

Setting her sights on an unimaginable journey across the Nullarbor Plain, Winifred was well and truly prepared, defying the many naysayers who told the 21-year-old she couldn't do it.

Winifred was 11 years old when she decided that she wanted a motorbike. Her parents laughed at the idea and only commented *"later dear",* but she was determined and when old enough gained her motorcycle licence and also bought her very first bike a 250cc BSA. Winifred practised

The striking face of Winifred Wells.

the art of scrambling (riding/racing across rough open ground) on her BSA which put her in good stead for her adventures ahead.

"I got thrown off the bike when a chap threw a 'Uey' in front of me and I went flying. I realised I needed to learn more about riding so I went to join the local club. And they didn't want me. Didn't want a woman. Typical male chauvinism!" (taken from interview with Winifred Wells, *Old Bike Australasia* issue 24).

A rarity in motorcycling society of late 1940s, she was young, she was female, but determined to prove her skill behind the bars. At this stage she changed up to a 350cc Triumph Tiger, a larger framed bike, which gave her a greater presence on the road and of course more power. Inevitably, Winifred convinced the club that she was a skilled motorcyclist and worthy of acceptance. The members of the club accepted her but also attempted to convince her that her dreams of crossing the Nullarbor would never eventuate. They told Winifred that *"she would blow her bike up, her metal bearings would self-destruct and she would perish!"*

Not deterred, the young adventurous and captivating woman approached the local Royal Enfield agency in Perth, Carlyle and Co., who realised the marketing possibilities of signing

Winifred was presented with a silver cup by the Enfield Cycle Co, England at the completion of her solo ride.

Winifred up to purchase the bike that would take her from Perth to Sydney and back, on her epic ride across the 'never-never'. The owner, Carl Cohen, obviously saw the potential that Winifred exuded and the determined spirit she possessed. However, he still concreted in the contract that the Royal Enfield Bullet 350 would only become hers upon final payment. Winifred had secured finance from IAG (Insurance Australia Group), but had to obtain permission from them to take the Enfield out of the state.

Setting off at noon, 26 December (Boxing Day) 1950 from Perth, Winifred was prepared. She had packed her provisions and spare clothing into pannier bags, a suitcase and a knapsack and in her pocket was £25.

Winifred's natural grace and style were captured beautifully in the numerous photographs that were taken as she departed. The black and white images were striking, however they did not capture the coloured charm of her fawn breeches, blue sweater and old tweed hat.

Beginning in the height of Australia's harsh summer, Winifred's immediate sights were set on the most intense part of her journey crossing *nullusarbor* (Latin) meaning *'no trees'*. Most of her journey was ridden in extreme heat, with only the most minimal of relief from the sun when she erected a shelter from her groundsheet and blanket or taking cover under the occasional structures that covered bore water holes. Her first day's journey took her to Southern Cross, approximately 231 miles (372 kms) from Perth. An average 366 miles (589 kms) per day and 95 miles per gallon was her goal, a mean feat considering the 350cc Royal Enfield Bullet averaged a top speed of approximately 70 miles (112.65 kms).

As the sun rose on the morning after reaching the edge of the Nullarbor Plain, so began the most gruelling part of her adventure. She continued on, reaching the town of Norseman safely on the evening of 27 December 1950. She had intended to continue onto Eucla that day, however, her motorbike skidded on some loose gravel 27 miles outside Coolgardie, which shook her to the core and she did not feel fit enough to press on, so she set up camp for the night. *"It was the loneliest hole you ever saw, but I wasn't scared."* The next day was her worst day. *"I was haring down these terrible corrugations and had the biggest spill you could imagine, a full locker and high side that sent me sprawling. It was near Spargoville, one of those small mining settlements that had sprung up in the goldfields, and a motorist tried to convince me to return to Perth. He was quite distressed because I'd wiped the side of my face off and cracked my head. I'd also done a bit of damage to the bike but the garage in Norseman gave me a bit of a hand with the bike and that was that."* (taken from interview with Winifred Wells, *Old Bike Australasia* issue 24).

On New Year's Day, Winifred rode into Adelaide to be given the warmest of welcomes by motorcycling enthusiasts, led by Mr. George Bolton of Bolton's Motorcycles Adelaide, being the Royal Enfield distributor.

Mr Bolton sent through a letter to the Royal Enfield headquarters in Redditch, England *"after having covered 1731 miles across arduous desert country in blazing heat, Miss Wells left Adelaide at 5 PM, for Melbourne and thence to Sydney, where she arrived at 6:15 PM on January 5. She spent a day there seeing the sights and began the return trip on January 7, leaving at 9:30 AM, and arriving back in Adelaide on January 10, having a day's rest in Melbourne. She covered the distance from Melbourne to Adelaide, 462 miles, between 6:30 AM and 7:20 PM. She left after 3 PM, on the 11th, carrying our best wishes and prayers that she would get through safely and achieve her desire to complete the journey within 21 days. Our hopes are high that this gallant little soul will win out. When she left Adelaide the temperature was 104.9° and, she travels south, so the thermometer rose, but she succeeded in reaching Port Augusta by 8 PM, having covered 204 miles."*

Capturing everyone's hearts, all involved waited with bated breath for any news of her sighting. Mr George Bolton phoned through to the police at Port Augusta, asking them to advise the other police officers along the track to look out for her in case of emergencies.

"Camped out at night in mid-desert, with her face scarred from a heavy fall in loose gravel, dust begrimed and mentally and physically tired, Winifred Wells had time to reflect on her hazardous ride. She never contemplated giving up, she says, and never thought that the long return trip — the first ever accomplished by a woman motor cyclist — would be cause for even casual comment except for her own family circle". (*People* Magazine – April 11, 1951)

Winifred had set out from Perth with only a few of her friends knowing her intention, however when she returned she was hailed Australia-wide as a heroine.

Winifred's arrival back in Perth being congratulated by the Lord Mayor.

George Bolton, Royal Enfield agent congratulates and celebrates Winifred and her father's arrival outside his premises in Adelaide South Australia.

"Winifred Wells arrived back in Perth 1 PM today. Congratulated by Lord Mayor completing meritorious riding, coast to coast and back in 21 days stop she is fit and well. Royal Enfield "Bullet" came through without missing a beat, engine running like a watch… Carlyle." (Telegram issued by Carlyle & Co).

"I did it just for the heck of it!", was Winifred Wells' response to a London journalist when she was asked why.

"To brave, alone, the barren, sandy, waterless ways of the Nullarbor Plains, a sparsely inhabited desert over 1000 miles wide, is an undertaking that, in itself, would test the huskiest male and, having done it once, few would care to repeat the dose; yet Winifred Wells made the crossing twice in three weeks." (*Motorcycling Magazine*, London February 8, 1951).

WINIFRED'S SOLO ITINERARY – 1950

December 26: left Perth at noon, spent night at Southern Cross (231 miles – 372 km)

December 27: reached Norseman (219 mile – 353 km)

December 28: rode 290 miles (466 km)

December 29: reached Eucla

December 30: reached Ceduna (305 mile – 492 km)

December 31: reached Port Augusta (284 mile – 457 km)

WINIFRED'S SOLO ITINERARY – 1951

January 1:   reached Adelaide 5:30 PM. (190 miles – 307 km)

               Winifred departed for Melbourne the same afternoon

January 2:   reached Melbourne (451 miles – 726 km)

January 3:   rested

January 4:   left for Sydney

January 5:   reached Sydney (545 miles – 878 km)

January 6:   rested

January 7:   left Sydney

January 8:   arrived Melbourne 8 am January 9: rested

January 10:   left Melbourne 7 am, arrived Adelaide 7pm. (451 miles – 726 km)

January 11:   left Adelaide 9:30 pm for Port Augusta

January 12:   reached Ceduna

January 13:   reached Eucla

January 14:   reached Norseman

January 15:   reached Southern Cross

January 16:   reached Perth 1 pm.

Two years on, the arduous but inspiring epic solo journey did not deter Winifred from more adventures. However, this time her father, Mr G Wells, was determined to accompany his young 23-year-old daughter on an even more challenging journey. Travelling from Perth to Darwin, Alice Springs, Tennant Creek, Mount Isa, Cairns, Charters Towers, Emerald, Townsville, Brisbane and down the New England highway to Newcastle.

The trip was full of adventure. The worst stretch was through the Kimberley Ranges in Western Australia, where they were continually fording creeks. When attempting to fill their water bags in the Northern Territory they were chased and charged several times by wild bulls.

WINIFRED AND GEORGE'S ITINERARY – 1952

September 23:   departed Perth

October 5:   arrived in Lagrange (Bidyadanga community) (1273 miles – 2050 km)

October 7:   Fitzroy Crossing (317 miles – 510 km)

October 14:   Darwin (917 miles – 1476 km)

October 20:   Mount Isa (994 miles – 1600 km)

October 24:   Cairns (725 miles – 1167 km)

November 3:   Brisbane (1046 miles – 1684 km)

November 6:   Newcastle (484 miles – 780 km)

November 7:   Sydney (106 miles – 170 km)

November 12:   Melbourne (546 miles – 879 km)

November 17:   Adelaide (452 miles – 727 km)

November 21:   Ceduna (483 miles – 777 km)

November 23:   Norseman (746 miles – 1201 km)

November 24:   Kalgoorlie (118 miles – 190 km)

November 26:   Perth (369 miles – 595 km)

The Argus newspaper of Melbourne (November 1952) announced ***"If your life is dull-try Winifred's remedy"*** … *"A lovely hot, foaming Bath was just what Winifred Wells, 23, of Perth wanted - and got - after riding a motorcycle here from Perth - the long way 'round, through Darwin".*

They arrived back in Perth on Wednesday, 26 November 1952 after having completed a motorcycle ride around Australia – travelling 10,000 miles.

To anyone following in her tire-tracks, Winifred warned *"Be prepared for plenty of punctures in north of Western Australia."*

Winifred's wonderful and much publicised adventures on her motorcycles concluded and Winifred slipped gracefully from the public spotlight with the knowledge that she did indeed achieve her dreams.

Photos supplied by George Bolton and The State Library of Western Australia

June Murray taking possession of her Matchless at AP Norths.

7

JUNE MURRAY

THE INSPIRATIONAL AND TREMENDOUSLY POPULAR REDEX TRIAL RIDER

"It is 2494 miles of 'murder' ", was the newspaper headline presented to 29-year-old June Murray, both introducing and enticing her to the challenge of the 1954 Australian Redex Reliability trial.

The Daily Telegraph (Sydney, New South Wales) edition of March 1954 was the first June knew of the life-changing event. Don Oxford, of the Central Motorcycle Club, arrived on June's doorstep, presenting the article to see if June *"really would"* go on the trial. June's husband Hilton, had put her name down as a member of the Matchless team, without consulting her first! *"Dad would initiate something, and subsequently Mum would succeed, often to the point where he was faced with her superiority! Not an easy situation for a man in those times! I remember his irritation (a euphemism for ire!) at being called "Mr June Murray" by his mates when all the publicity about the Redex came out".* (Cynthia Atkin- daughter).

June was born on 18th April 1925 in Byron Bay, NSW, into a family of four boys and three girls. She had always wanted a motorcycle and her passion was beautifully captured in an image of her riding the New England Highway in the autumn of 1942, on a Triumph 500cc (belonging to her future husband Hilton Murray). June was 17 at the time and by the time she had reached 21, she and Hilton had given birth to three daughters.

"On her own she raised my two sisters and myself, while my father was doing his duty as a despatch rider in the war years. Mum taught herself to type on a Royal typewriter. She then got a position as secretary with A.F Morgan and Sons Pty Ltd (a large plumbing company in Mosman Sydney, NSW). Mum also worked as an usherette at the Narrabeen movie theatre, on Thursday, Friday and Saturday nights. The late 1940s and 1950s were post Second World War years. During this time there was very little money around or jobs. Both my mother and father had two jobs each. My dad was a diesel engineer and he also worked in a company called Pyrex (a glass manufacturer) as a product quality control inspector. Both my parents were hard-working conscientious people. This was to help them educate, feed and put a roof over our heads." (Judith Zielinski - daughter).

Motorcycling was a family affair for the Murrays, with their three young daughters, Cynthia, Judith and Susan, joining them at motorcycling events. The girls helped with oiling the chains, push starting bikes and helping unload their trailer for Sunday race events. As children were not allowed in the pits, the girls would watch their dad racing for a while, then when they got bored, as kids do, they would walk around picking up empty milk and cordial bottles, returning them to the kiosk as a boost to their pocket money. The three girls also sold programmes at the gate.

Hilton was a fanatic, owning up to 13 motorbikes at one time, and while he raced at Mount Druitt, Bathurst, Wallacia, Frenchs Forest and Holdsworthy Army track in Liverpool, June would often be in the tower scoring laps.

June was a natural rider and loved the freedom felt on two wheels. She regularly rode to her job as a secretary, picking one of the girls up from school (much to their embarrassment, as having a motorcycling mother in the 1950s was not normal) and competing in events on weekends, including the Goodwin Shield Trial. The bike that AP North Pty. Ltd. (the Matchless Dealership, located in Sydney, NSW) gave June to ride in the Redex was brand new and in those days and all new vehicles had to be "run in". This meant not pushed above a certain speed for a specified distance, which would give the engine time to loosen up. The only way she could "run the bike in" was to ride from her home in Collaroy Plateau to the Hawkesbury River, NSW, at night, after the girls were in bed, a ride of at least an hour each way.

June with fellow competitors after the Redex Trial.

*June ready to start
the Redex Trial*

June always maintained her own bike, changing its tyres, de-coking the engine to remove carbon build up, regrinding the valves and changing rings. Honing her skills proved valuable, equipping her well for future events.

June and Hilton became members of the Central Motorcycle Club of Sydney, Manly-Warringah Motorcycle Club and Racing Riders Motorcycle Club. As June wasn't officially recognised by the clubs (at the time women were not allowed to officially compete) she attended all the events but was relegated to ride behind.

However, by 1951 June's achievements were being recognised.

"One of the most commendable performances of this year's Goodwin Shield was that of the lone lady competitor, Mrs. June Murray. This grand sportswoman was contesting her second Goodwin Shield. In 1951, when conditions were much better than this year, this enthusiastic motor cyclist completed the course, this time for a loss of 138 points. In the 1952 edition, under extreme conditions, she again completed the course, this time for a loss of only 73 points. When it is taken into consideration that this gallant lady is the mother of three children, and battled her way through the entire distance, whilst many men retired from the event before negotiating half the distance, the Auto Cycle

Union could do far worse than present Mrs. Murray with a trophy for a very gallant effort."

And

"In our last issue we suggested that our only lady Trials rider should receive some recognition by the A.C.U. for her splendid performance in the 1952 Goodwin Shield. The Matter was brought to the fore at the last general meeting by Mr. Harry Bartrop. Result: A trophy for Mrs. Murray."

Also

"Another to display the courage and perseverance we know our sport brings to the fore, was Mrs. Murray who, though taking a toss lost points on the first days, but turned up at the social on Saturday night."

"Mrs. Murray, of the Central M.C.C, will again try her luck in the Goodwin Shield. This enthusiastic Trials rider never misses a competition of this nature, and now becomes the sole lady entrant in NSW competition. We raise our hats to a grand sport."

Then

"Popular June Murray (Central) arrived at the start well prepared to do battle for her club, but, alas, no support, so June was prevailed upon not to start. How do you MEN feel about that?"

(quotes taken from monthly journal/newsletters put out by the motorcycle clubs 1951/52)

The Central Motorcycle Club team was a major entrant in the Redex trial of 1954. Matchless and BSA (*"Bloody Sore Arse"* – June Murray 2015) teams were entered. June was a celebrated and consistent competitor for the Central Motorcycle Club, so it followed that June represented her club.

The Redex was an exciting, enthralling, challenging but incredibly dangerous event. 2494 miles (4013 km) through New South Wales, South Australia and Victoria. Not for the faint hearted, the trial was laced with snow, rain, mud, gale-force winds, desert, bulldust, culverts, extreme cold, unsealed roads, kangaroos, and sand banks.

June was prepared! AP North gave June a 350cc motorcycle to ride the event. Hilton made her map holder, Berlei donated a pair of underpants and a bra, Angus and Coote donated a watch, her brother dressed her in leather clothing, and supplied panniers and a lap rug.

Amidst a swarm of media, June Murray – number 22 – departed on the Redex Reliability Trial, from Parramatta Park, Sydney on Sunday 6th June 1954. In the foreground were her proud parents who had travelled from Mona Vale to Parramatta, a long distance in those days, to farewell their daughter. However, the officials prevented them coming onto the road and they had to be content to call out goodbye.

"My only recollection I have of mum's courageous endeavours in the Redex Trial was that my two sisters (Cynthia, 11 years old, and Susan, 8 years old) were sitting on a dais at Parramatta Park. We had our photos taken for the newspaper. That's the only thing I remember about the start of the trial. When mum left on the trial, dad took us up to Cessnock (the first check point) in our Austin A40 car. We met mum and dad checked the bike and spoke to mum about her riding." (Judith Zielinski – daughter).

AP North's Redex Team.

The only other female competitor was Miss Joyce Aylmer, who rode a Jawa 250cc bike as a member of the Bruce Small team from Melbourne, Victoria.

With secret control spots known only to officials, competitors were forced to maintain steady average speeds, rarely higher than 45 mph or lower than 25 mph. If the riders arrived at the control spots earlier or later than the set schedule they would lose valuable points. And if the rider's motorcycle was found to be without the key parts officially stamped before the start, they would be disqualified. There was an official river crossing with competitors being advised (tongue in cheek!) that if they didn't like the idea, they were entitled to fell a tree and ride across it, or strap the bike to their back and swim across.

AP North's Redex Team.

"The worst time for me was riding across the desert from Broken Hill. I was travelling alone and was frightened I would get lost in those thousands of tracks."

Near Burra, South Australia, June's Matchless struck gravel and threw her off. She was unharmed, although the windscreen and headlight glass were broken.

"June Murray was wonderful. Near Jingellic I saw her fall from her Matchless time and time again. Sometimes she was on the point of crying, but battled on."
(Miss Joyce Aylmer).

The very last stretch of the trial tackled the steep terrain of the Blue Mountains coming down the other side into Parramatta and the much-welcomed finish line. Race protocol determined that riders were sent off each morning in the order they had come into the control point on the previous night. June had come close to last the night before and knew that she would be among the last riders to leave the next morning. No worries – she was determined to finish! She found out later that one of the riders had gone to the organisers and asked if June could be sent off among the lead group so that she would have riders behind her who could help if she got into difficulties. June knew nothing of this at the time.

"I think that is a beautiful story and a tribute to Mum and the relationship she had with everybody in the riding community." (Cynthia Atkin – daughter).

June registering for the Redex Trial.

107 MOTORCYCLISTS DEPARTED AND 71 FINISHED

THE OFFICIAL PLACINGS:

Keith. Stewart, of Bankstown (Matchless) – No points lost (Monica Stewart's husband Chapter 5)

R. Dungate, of Blakehurst – 1 point lost

E. Hinton, of Belfields (Norton) – 1 point lost

W. Mayes, of Rydalmere (BSA) – 2 points (Hazel Maye's husband Chapter 4)

And

June Murray – 600 points lost

Joyce Aylmer – 1000 points lost

"Dear Mrs. Murray, on reading through accounts of the recent Redex Trial it seems hardly possible that anyone bar the hardiest of Motor Cyclists could have negotiated such an arduous route as you so ably did on your Model G3LS Matchless, and I have the greatest pleasure, on behalf of us all in the Matchless Organisation, in extending to you our very hearty congratulations on such a fine effort.

When we read of your particularly bad experiences during the Trial, and then noted your statement to reporters at the end that "I'll have another go at it next year", we knew how it was that you managed to check in at the final control – sheer tenacity in spite of all difficulties.

We all wish you every success in future events and may you enjoy many more years of happy Motor Cycling on a Matchless.

Yours sincerely G. G. Scott"

(28/7/1954, Matchless Motor Cycles London)

Post-race, June outshone the race winners and was the flavour of the month for the Australian media, with numerous newspaper and magazine interviews. The *Australian Women's Weekly*, in April of 1954, posted the headline, "Mother contests motor-cycle race – She finds de-coking bike easier than making kiddies' dresses" describing June to be the "Only" woman entrant in the Redex.

The one event that stole the limelight from Mrs June Murray was the Petrov Affair (the defection of two Russian spies to Australia).

June was named by The Women's International Motorcycling Association (based in the USA) the **World's Most Outstanding Woman Rider of 1954**. She received a congratulatory letter from the President who described her efforts as "magnificent" and a trophy in the form of a golden robed woman with wings. An appropriate tribute to June who had certainly gained her wings within the motorcycling fraternity.

The only Redex Reliability Motorcycle Trial was held in 1954. However, this did not stop June and her passion for Trial riding, going on to compete in the 1956 Caltex Oil Trial, riding her Velocette L.E (little engine) MII (water-cooled, 192cc) motorcycle.

In 1959, June Murray gave up trial riding and motorcycling when the family moved from Collaroy Plateau to Arcadia Vale NSW, but never gave up her active life, taking up Ten Pin Bowls and Lawn Bowls.

"Mum is now unable to do the wonderful things she did in her youth. My mother is an amazing and remarkable woman. I love and cherish her fantastic, interesting life. She has done many things that women could aspire to and achieve" (Judith Zielinski – daughter).

At the ripe age of 91, even in the midst of dementia, June still has beautiful flashes of her remarkable achievements that have secured her place in Australia's history books.

"Oh, car driving is dull. On a bike there's a feeling of power and control." (June Murray).

Photos supplied by Cynthia Atkin – Daughter,
and Jim Scaysbrook – Old Bike Australasia.

June competing in the 1956 Caltex Oil Trial.

8

PEGGY HYDE

THE FIRST WOMAN IN THE WORLD TO BE GRANTED AN UNRESTRICTED ROAD RACING LICENCE

In early 1962 Peggy Hyde was a trail-blazer in the true sense of the word. As a young music student Peggy never imagined that in just a few short years, she would become a world first, leading the way for women to race unrestricted capacity motorcycles and to compete in world class race events.

As a 10-year-old child, not yet interested in motorcycles, Peggy did however passionately desire to ride a pushbike. A neighbour had paused at the front gate of her family home to chat with her mother – a child in tow, with pushbike. Whilst the mothers were chatting and not attending to their daughters the scene was set. *"Hence my hurried exit, having quietly organised a ride with the child 'owner' of the pushy!"* Peggy's mother screaming, *"Come back, you'll be killed!"* Peggy pedalled away as fast as she could. *"Oh what fun!"* This was Peggy's first taste of the exhilaration and freedom felt on two wheels.

Early photographs of Peggy's father, who passed away when she was nine, show him driving a sidecar outfit. However, motorcycling was certainly not part of her family life and upbringing. Her only early experience was being given a ride in a sidecar belonging to a friend's father. Peggy was not particularly impressed!

Peggy bought her first motorbike in early 1963, whilst studying at the Melbourne University and Conservatory of Music. A few months later, Peggy's left wrist was crushed when a careless car driver made a

Left: Peggy Hyde.

U-turn in front of her without signalling. Despite this serious setback, she continued her studies and helped pay her way by working as a commercial despatch rider, on scooters and motorbikes. Five collisions in six weeks, due to a scooter with no brakes quelled her enthusiasm for poorly-maintained scooters but did not quell her enthusiasm for two wheels.

Those early years dealing with Melbourne traffic, braking and cornering, the wet slippery oil laden inner city streets and unmade outer suburban roads inadvertently taught Peggy fundamental skills. With nothing in mind other than using the cheapest form of transport to carry her to her position as Choirmaster and church organist, Peggy's lifelong love affair with motorcycles was about to begin.

Approaching a local scooter shop in the Elizabeth Street motorcycle hub of Melbourne she was greeted by a keen salesman advising that *"girls ride scooters"*. Realising that the salesman was prejudiced and that he had a vested interest in selling her a scooter, she moved onto a motorcycle dealership to be given the same response, *"girls ride scooters."* In Peggy's mind both dealerships had just done themselves out of a sale. Not to be defeated, and now possessing simmering determination, Peggy marched out of the shop, up a side lane to Keith 'Dutchy' Holland's motorcycle repair shop, where again she was told *"girls ride scooters."* Peggy, now mentally prepared for this same unqualified response asked "Why?" His answer was simple, *"I have no idea really!"* Then Peggy asked, *"So what's safer?"* and he said, *"A motorbike"*. So that is what Peggy bought, a 350cc Matchless single cylinder motorcycle purchased for 55 pounds.

"My first ride on it was spectacular, opened the throttle and dropped the clutch, in the gravel, leaving the road and veering off into the scrub, I did emerge the victor, having immediately discovered that when feeling unstable the best thing to do is to open the throttle some more. It was probably lucky that there were enough gaps between trees, and that scrubby stuff was not thick, as I got control and returned to the dirt road I'd started on, having gravel blasted the friend who had elected to help me learn to ride. This was (later) my husband. WHAT FUN!!! And I was 'hooked'."

It was not long before Peggy realized that motorcycling was not only economical but also fun **and she was good at it.**

When Peggy first met Julian Hyde he had had a run in with a car on his Jawa 250cc, which resulted in a bandaged sorry sight when Peggy first met him at 'The Horse Market Hotel' (a popular student hang-out), where she had asked around for assistance in buying a motorcycle.

The old house in Carlton, where Peggy lived with five other students, became a haven for motorcycles. One count put the number at 13. Says Peggy: "Not to be outdone, everyone bought at least one bike each, and we used to swap." (The *Australian Women's Weekly* 21 June 1972). Dubbed the *'Melbourne Uni Motorcycle Putsch'* [1] (by Ric Begg, a fellow student and rider) her social riding life expanded.

Peggy's riding prowess was enhanced by experiencing many different riding styles and surfaces, participating in many formal and informal events including hill climbs, trials, sand racing, and trail riding (including on a Norton 750cc). She rode off road a lot, always on road tyres and without footing; mainly because she couldn't reach the ground and it hurt her back to try.

Upgrading from Matchless and Ariel 350cc and 500cc, Peggy naturally progressed to a much larger machine, a 750cc Norton Atlas, which famously carried her on a solo adventure in 1964 from Melbourne, Victoria to Marlborough, Queensland and back. She rode the Norton in all conditions taking the challenge of riding through bulldust every day near her home and once getting trapped between rocks in the Grampians National Park in Victoria.

"I loved riding anywhere, often took off with only the foggiest notion of where I was going, seldom looked at a map, typically got fuel at corner service stations, came in on the highway entrance and left via the side road exit, waking up 80 miles later I was out of fuel again and not on the highway. Slept in funny places, met interesting people."

Media interest in Peggy's adventures began early in her riding career. In 1964, Peggy effortlessly rode her Norton Atlas 750cc, *'a large one for a woman to handle'* as quoted in The *Maryborough Chronicles*, from Melbourne throughout country NSW, having to detour from her planned route to Sydney to have a cracked cylinder repaired. The next morning, she moved on from Sydney and arrived in Warwick Queensland (778.1 km) on the same day.

1 Putsch – an attempt to overthrow a government, a coup.

Peggy Hyde taking on and out in front of the legendry Ken Blake.

'Despite a warning on the state of the weather, she left Maryborough yesterday, with skies darkened by approaching storm clouds… that did not appear to worry her, and smiling she accepted it all with the determined "I'll give it a go" spirit.' (from *The Maryborough Chronicles*).

Peggy and Julian Hyde went on to join the local Hartwell motorcycling club. Peggy decided that club road runs weren't for her, Peggy did not like being slipstreamed and she preferred riding faster on winding roads. Peggy wanted to race! At first her interest was scrambling, but by the time she was thinking of preparing a bike to race, Matchless had become outdated by new brands. That left road racing, where she could ride her own bike, at this time the Norton. **She was a natural at riding and road racing became a natural extension of her experience to date.**

As motorcycle technology improved dramatically and machines that were considered 'high-powered' in the 1960s were overtaken by more powerful motorcycles, the racing world thrived. Not so for women! The perception then was that a woman simply could not handle the weight and power of higher capacity machines. **Peggy Hyde proved the world wrong**!

What Peggy didn't know was that racing licences were issued to women only to enter bikes, not to race them. Race licences were required for both entrants and riders in the 1960s. When applying for her licence Peggy omitted to tick the two boxes that determined you to be either a race entrant or competitor (an entrant is the owner of the motorcycle. The competitor is the rider of the motorcycle. A competitor can also be an entrant if the motorcycle she or he is riding is her/his own registered motorcycle). This went unnoticed by Licencing Authorities and an unrestricted Victorian Open Competition Licence was granted.

Late in 1966 when Peggy started racing there were *no* women racing. Her local club, Hartwell Motorcycle Road Racing Club, was supportive; they had ridden with her on the road. It was crucial to her future access to the track that this first race report be unbiased. The Club secretary, a woman (Ruth Love) knew that if the track officials realised Peggy was a woman, her first performance would be criticised unfairly, to keep her off the track. The Club organising team kept the secret and assisted by publishing only surnames and initials of riders.

Peggy and Julian parked their van far from other competitors and officials, rode the same bike, wore the same leathers and changed out of view. So, combined with the assumption that a woman would only be an entrant, and that women were not expected to be seen on the race track, officials and spectators simply assumed that M.J. Hyde (Peggy's birth name being Margaret) and J.P. Hyde were in fact brothers.

'M.J. Hyde's' post-race steward's reports were good, quickly moving her up from D-grade to C-Grade. Two more race meetings followed quickly, but being run by other clubs, Peggy's gender was no longer a secret. When she applied for her annual licence renewal, she was issued a licence restricted to 250cc. After an initial exchange of correspondence with the Auto Cycle Council of Australia stating her case that there was no basis for any restriction because she was not a Junior and her steward reports were good. She added *'could it be because the Victorian Committee were all men?'* Peggy said that it was not so much that she was doing it for the women's libbers, she just wanted what was fair: there was no rational reason for excluding women from open competition or restricting what they could ride.

In 1969 a prompt response and apology from the National Council followed with the granting of an unrestricted racing licence and a new policy permitting women to compete on machines of any size. **Peggy at that stage did not realise she was the first woman in the world to hold such a licence.**

Peggy's natural talent was seldom reflected in the media of the day with her finding many of the journalists "rather irritating" and some "rather well meaning", always with the comment that she handled her machine "like a man". Journalist Lance Lowe for *The Open Road* (1 March 1970) in his article entitled **"Brown-eyed blonde beats 90 men"** details his description of Peggy's *"Vital Statistics"* (her bust-waist-hip measurements). Lowe went on to partially salvage the credibility of his work by documenting Peggy Hyde's many talents describing Peggy as astute and *"in contrast to her average male enthusiast who tends to become completely absorbed in his racing and tuning world, she also has other activities as widely diverse as raising pedigreed goats and studying music. She plays the piano, is an accomplished pipe organist and has one subject to pass at the Melbourne Conservatorium of Music to gain her Bachelor of Music Degree. Her Toggenburg goats are famous in*

Peggy in the pits riding the Castrol 6 hour event.

Peggy Hyde riding again at the Broadford Motorcycle Complex, Victoria 2015.

Victoria and successful at agricultural shows. As if all this is not enough, Mrs Hyde also has a full-time job-delivering automotive spare parts for a Melbourne car company."

When one journalist expressed his concern that she may hurt herself in an event, Peggy's response was that she *"was sure she would heal exactly as a man would"*. Whispers came from some in the media even questioning if Peggy was indeed a woman, leading to Peggy reluctantly allowing a photo of her in a bikini to be published.

Peggy maintained her composure and always graciously and calmly responded to media scrutiny. **At this stage and omitted in media reports was the fact that Peggy was the first woman in Australia to win an open road race.**

"I won my first race – C grade Unlimited – in 1969 at Phillip Island- a runaway win. Great fun, on my Mach III (the very first model Kawasaki 500cc H1 two-stroke triple, a truly remarkable beast. My mother was there to see it. *Later that day, against stronger competition, I lapped faster……"*

Following this win Peggy was asked by the Holden car racing team if she would consider driving for them. She declined, in favour of motorbike racing.

By 1970 Peggy had won nine events on her Kawasaki Mach III 500cc three-cylinder motorcycle. The 26-year-old Peggy was *"Victoria's Wonder Woman"* orchestrating her moves on the most accomplished and awarded racers of the time. Peggy never bowed. She held firm and with belief in her own ability, racing counterparts fell like bowling pins as she wove her path through tight turns, wet surfaces and mechanical hiccups. Much to the amusement of some of the older and wiser competitors (one jesting "If you beat me again I'll retire!"), Peggy outgunned the young guns who were riding the most modern of motorcycles. She created history at Phillip Island, Victoria, by winning the Senior C grade race on her Kawasaki 500, becoming the first woman in Australia to win a road race and also qualifying her to run in the Senior and Unlimited Tourist Trophy (T/T) title events where she finished third. *"Lap two she took the lead from Jones and then, trying to save face for the male sex, he slid off on the thwird lap to retire. From then on Hyde had two seconds from Blake, who made a desperate attempt on the last lap to regain male honour but went down too, coming off at Shell Corner!"* (*Australian Motorcycle News*, 1 May 1970 edition). Ken Blake was ranked number one and Peter Jones number two in Australian racing in 1970. In incessant pursuit she hunted down the next mark. Peggy's desire was not driven by the glory of first place, only by the chase. *"I rode for fun"* she said.

When Oran Park organisers asked Peggy to ride in a new, women only class called 'The Powder Puff Derby', she refused at first. *"After all I'd done to ensure equality for women on the track, here they were trying to set us apart again.*

Insulting women as "powder puffs", too. At the same time, I realised that women who didn't want to race with men might think I was being separatist from other women. So in the end I agreed to ride in the women's race as well as in the Open races. In subsequent women's races the organisers set me handicaps or asked me to ride slowly. Before the last of these races they'd run out of ideas and asked to "make it look like a race". I practised in the pits – stalling the bike (clutch start) with a planned loss of 7 seconds. On the grid however half a dozen official pushers descended on me, delaying my get-away. I still won. Afterwards a reporter came up to me – "you stalled the bike! I saw you put your foot on the brake!" he said; "but you're not going to publish that" I said, and he didn't."

The following year, in 1971, Peggy and Julian moved to Sydney, New South Wales. They purchased land to continue their goat farming business where Peggy thrived. In 1975, her life and her world that had become immersed in motorcycle racing, changed. Dairy farming was full-on heavy physical work. Her husband Julian was losing interest in racing. Although he kept his own bike, he eventually persuaded Peggy to sell her last bike, her beloved Kawasaki 900 Z1. Her last participant badge was for Bathurst 1975. She felt very sorry to give up her last motorcycle, and even sorrier to see that the bike wasn't being cared for by the new owner as well as she'd have liked.

Peggy and Julian separated in 1979. Peggy continued farming for a short time. Getting off the farm was a difficult process. By then she was back at University doing a Graduate Diploma in Education for secondary school teaching, unfortunately undergoing major surgery – for the third time in 10 years. By then she had been introduced to sailing. Her first sail was just like her first ride on a motorbike – she was hooked. In a sense the pushbike, the motorcycle and the yacht became one. In 1983 she "went sailing", caught the trade winds, and after years cruising the Queensland coast she found herself in Townsville where she has lived on her beloved yacht ever since. Studying again, this time for an Honours degree in Social Science in Psychology, she worked as a registered psychologist until retirement. During this time, she became a conservation activist and lobbyist leading the Hinchinbrook campaign for many years, working on a voluntary basis for NGO (Non-government organisation) groups and sitting on government committees.

Her skill, her story, and her memorable form never dulled in the minds of motorcycle enthusiasts and the question *'Where is Peggy Hyde now?'* regularly surfaced in social media. In 2014 and at the age of 71, Peggy renewed her racing licence "only 38 years out of date at the time" and gracefully returned to the world of motorcycling. "I'm looking forward now to another historic replay".

After her long absence it was one of her despatch riding mates Ric Begg (Melbourne Uni Motorcycle Putsch) who recognised her at Broadford 2014 Classic event, welcoming her back with *"Peggy! Got a ride yet? Take my 1000…"* She was invited back into the historic racing scene with open arms, starting with Phillip Island January 2015, the track where she had won her first race on an early model Kawasaki Mach III 500cc triple (H1). Ric had organised a 1972 model H1B and Peggy was back on the track. She hadn't been on a bike at all in 33 years.

The following year, 2015, flowed with numerous invitations to race events and interviews and the fervour extended by the motorcycling community reflects the great respect and admiration Peggy received from her gracious professionalismon the track.

Peggy Hyde is still racing… *"For road racing in particular you don't need to have brute strength when it comes to judgement and understanding what's happening, it's silly to think that women would be less competent."* Peggy Hyde

A determined and passionate spirit resides in her frame and it is this spirit that created the legend that is Peggy Hyde.

Photos supplied by: Peggy Hyde, Jim Scaysbrook – Old Bike Australasia and Neil Binnion

9

LINDA BOOTHERSTONE-BICK

THE UNEQUIVOCAL OVERLANDER

"Forget all the images painted by media, and open your heart and mind to the world. A smile is the only weapon expedient in the pack of an overlander." (from song The Overlander written by Linda Bootherstone-Bick).

Before we embark on following Linda Bootherstone-Bick's adventures we need to know a few vital facts! Linda started her two-wheeled circumnavigation of the world when she was 18, then spent her 20s, 30s, 40s, 50s, 60s and 70s experiencing the highs and lows of the terra firma beneath the two wheels of her motorcycles, in some of the most challenging and remote places on the earth.

Be it on dirt, sand, gravel or asphalt, Linda has joyously transversed the globe on her motorcycles for nigh on 60 years.

Linda has an uncanny ability to transcend all the major challenges of a riding experience, be it uncertain road and weather conditions, her motorcycle's health and well-being or dodging erratic four-wheeled road users, to name a few – but also, the minor ones including the logistics of ship transport between countries, the frightfully boring paperwork and the challenging language barriers that were part and parcel of the adventure.

In 2014, realising that her 70th birthday was the following year, she decided that she would like to

Left: Linda ready for her adventure – note Africa on her tank

be in Sucre, Bolivia with her musician friends to have a birthday that would equal the excitement of her 60th, celebrated high in the Himalayas whilst on her overland trip to Australia in 2005. She contacted her friends in Sucre saying she would arrive on the 21st November by motorcycle with her tin whistle and lager phone ready to celebrate and play music with them.

Their initial reply *was "you will suffer from the high altitudes and you will get sick", "the roads are really too bad for a motorbike"or "it's too cold, too wet and the terrain is too harsh!"* Yet Linda learned to ride motorbikes in 1963, and most of the travelling that Linda had done in her life had been on motorcycles, so her friend's comments did not deter her.

When asked what brought her to motorcycling in the first place this was her reply:

"My elder sister, Anne, had a boyfriend with a beautiful BSA Gold Star which fascinated me (and so did he, but to no avail)".

Her teenaged entry to freedom on wheels came in the form of a three wheeled Bond Minicar which she purchased out of her pocket money and her father helped rebuild. It was the oddest looking little car with one wheel at the front and two wheels at the back and a rather enthralling skull and crossbones emblazoned on the bonnet. This little car had the unlikely title Hiroshima II. Linda and her school friend, Lynn Filmore toured the south-west of England in the Bond and whilst gracing the open roads, the two friends met a couple of likely lads on motorcycles who invited the two young women for a ride. Sitting on the pillion pad was a short-lived experience for Linda as her pilot took a bend too fast and she ended up in hospital with concussion and cracked ribs.

"From then on I decided that I would take all bike riding into my own hands, joined the Saltbox Motorcycle Club in Biggin Hill near the famous World War II airfield, and bought my own bike. This was a 250 BSA C10L upon which Lynn and I learnt to ride. Unfortunately, during one of her outings a gentleman in a Rover made a wrong turn, Lynn ended up on the bonnet and the bike needed new forks. Having saved my sixpences (in a Dimple whiskey bottle) I lashed out its contents, all of £40, on a Triumph 200cc Tiger Cub and made several attempts at getting further than

the North Circular road but the bike's habit of throwing big ends deterred me so I graduated in to a Triumph 3TA which easily transported me to the Lake District and North Wales. A great little bike, it would do 90 mile-per-hour with 70 mile-per- gallon."

It was not long before Linda discovered the joy of cross-continent adventure, riding aboard her next bike, a Triumph 500cc 5TA motorcycle which she had re-painted "go-faster Bonneville blue". This bike delivered her to many motorcycle rallies in the UK and Europe, including the Dragon Rally (held only for the brave of heart during winter in North Wales), the Chamois (a summertime gathering at high altitude in the French Alps), the Stella Alpina (taking place in the Italian Alps riding in some of the most challenging terrain, quite often riding on gravel tracks through snow) and the 1967 Fédération Internationale de Motocyclisme (FIM) Rally in Moscow. This rally was very significant in confirming Linda's growing belief that motorcycling helped break down many international barriers. In that year, 1967, Russia was behind the Iron curtain, controlled by Khrushchev, and it was very difficult to travel there. Invitations for the FIM rally were issued to enable participants to acquire visas to enter and all of them had to follow strict rules while travelling in the country, escorted by tourist guides. However, sharing vodka and caviar in the gracious buildings in Moscow with the rally organizers and other east European participants was a great example of international friendship, despite language and cultural differences. The motorcycles were a common link.

Whilst attending the FIM Rally Linda met a couple of Aussie guys who were touring the world on BMWs. *"I travelled with one of them to the Troll Rally in Norway the following year and noted that, while he sat back and boiled the billy each night, I was still busy adjusting my chain and screwing up all the bolts that had loosened during the day's ride. This proved to me that BMWs needed less maintenance than Triumphs so I bought a 1960 R60 and took it with me on the ship when I immigrated to Oz in 1969. Unloading it in Melbourne I rode it across to Adelaide and then back east to Sydney, stopping at the Kangaroo Rally in Ballarat."* Linda came to Australia as a 'Ten pound Pom' and it didn't take her long to find her circle of motorcycling friends and to also expand her motorcycling disciplines. Living in Sydney in 1970, she and her flatmates, Jacky and Angie Griffin, befriended

Entering the desert.

the members of the Willoughby Motorcycle Club and the University of NSW Motorcycle club and it was here that she was introduced to racing. The 1970 Powder Puff Derby enticed Linda to the Oran Park Raceway with Ryans of Parramatta, a motorcycle dealership, lending her a 250 Suzuki Savage. They had been sponsors in a Road Safety Run event in which Linda had won best Solo and best Team with sisters Sandra and Deirdre Davis. Linda raced against the world's pioneering road racer Peggy Hyde (see Chapter 8).

In the same year, Linda and her friends moved on from Sydney, heading for the Nullarbor Plain – with their sights set on working in Perth before taking another tour around the Great Southern Land. Upon their arrival in Perth Linda dabbled again in racing, riding a borrowed Ducati 250 Desmo at Wanneroo Park and also traded her BMW R60 for the first brand new vehicle that she had ever owned, a BMW R60/5. The *'Three Wandering Poms'* (book published by Linda Bootherstone and Angela and Jacky Griffin) headed back to Sydney, then on to Cairns, Townsville, inland to Tennant Creek, north to Darwin, then back to Alice Springs where they put themselves and their bikes on the Ghan (train) and returned to Adelaide.

Finance for Linda's adventures never came easily and she always worked hard to save money before she would depart. For example, before leaving England for Africa, Linda held down three jobs at once to finance this journey. She also worked in different countries to extend her trips. With many strings to her bow, Linda is a talented musician, artist, poet, author, storyteller and, of course, an accomplished motorcyclist. She has a degree in Geography, Anthropology and History, a TEFL teaching qualification and is blessed with the gift of the gab "to boot". No wonder Linda successfully finds employment and accolades in many diverse parts of the world.

Linda's father took ill in 1974. This saw her return to the UK post-haste to be at his side, when he passed away Linda stayed on to assist her mother. Her dreams of travelling and riding throughout Canada slowly dissolved as the months went by and her plans for a motorcycle adventure during a Canadian winter were not a realistic option. Sunshine was in order, so she contacted the Automobile Association in England in the hope of obtaining literature on Africa. They advised her "DON'T!" Not deterred, Linda soldiered on in pursuit of her new adventure. At the time there was no travel information on Africa, no travel books, no Lonely Planet and certainly no Google, but Linda really liked to have surprise in her adventures and was happy to go with the flow. It was a time when few people ventured to Africa and there certainly weren't any other adventure motorcyclists there. It took her a few months to prepare, purchasing a 1957 BMW R50 which she kitted up, packed spares and then headed for the African continent. During her 15 month trip her BMW suffered broken suspension in the Sahara, shot main bearings in Kenya, dropped a valve in Rhodesia, cracked a piston in South Africa and picked up a puncture in the middle of a game park where she really wasn't meant to be; Linda suffered malaria, tackled Sahara sand and Congo mud while still keeping a smile on her face. (*"Into Africa with A Smile"*- Linda Bootherstone-Bick).

In England during the 60s Linda had become a member of the Women's International Motorcycle Association, a worldwide organisation with members in over 20 countries. *"I was interested in meeting its founder, Louise Scherbyn in America so, in 1983 (while living in Australia) I flew there and toured on a 360T Honda twin which she had*

In Kano, Nigeria.

arranged for me to buy from another member. A great little bike, its only fault was blowing main fuses which was rather inconvenient when overtaking other vehicles on the freeways. After 4 months I sold it for the same price I bought it for (about $400) when I flew back to Oz." After meeting Louise and many other friendly and helpful WIMA members in USA, Linda decided to found WIMA Australia in 1985.

Linda lived happily in South Australia for the best part of 15 years. During this time, she worked in the outback in isolated areas as part of a Community Arts Team and learnt skills in teaching art music and drama which were to help her in later projects. When her long-term relationship broke up she moved back to the UK, then, using her R60/7 shipped over from Australia, she rode through Italy and down to Malta with another woman as pillion, to help with a boating project. While the other two women sailed the yacht down the Mediterranean, she shipped her bike to Marseille and then rode down through Spain to meet them in Gibraltar. When her involvement with the project finished she stayed on in Spain where she spent the next 16 years, buying and renovating two goat herder's cottages, one to live in and the other to use for holiday rentals for touring motorcyclists or musicians. She used her BMW to take other women friends on guided tours of Morocco and attended many rallies in Spain, Portugal and Germany and another in Odessa, Ukraine. She wrote and performed cultural shows in language schools in Spain to help finance her trips. Her book, *Where Angels Fear to Tread* by Linda Bootherstone, describes her life over this period.

Her adventures continued with a 60th birthday trip – 21 months, 26 countries and 81,000 km! Starting in southern Spain, departing April 2005, Linda rode her Suzuki 650cc, through Europe, Turkey, Iran, Pakistan, India, Nepal and then flew the bike to Bangkok in Thailand and continued through Asia arriving back in Australia, January 2007. Many expressed their concerns for Linda when she was travelling alone asking *"A woman by herself, in strange countries such as Pakistan and Iran?"* But Linda was always treated very well, finding Islamic culture very hospitable. She was always shown the utmost respect and had no problems. She believed that this was because she was an older woman.

Linda in Central Africa.

Linda's overland adventures are very special to her because of the hospitality offered to her by complete strangers, Iranians offering to pay for her hotel bills and food, enthusiastic bikers in India arranging for her board and lodgings, and Asians extending warmth, food and a warm bed in their homes. *"This proves that people-to-people relationships transcend politics. I thought Bush was going to blow up Iran and Pakistan while I was halfway through those countries. But the hospitality of the people there was something special."*

Linda in Chile.

After her epic journey to Australia from Europe, Linda returned to Spain to sell her houses and, realising that South America was one of the last continents to visit, she bought a 250cc bike in North America with the intention of riding it down into the southern countries. Unfortunately, ill health prevented her completing this trip and she flew from Louisiana to Australia, leaving the bike behind to be later transported to the place where she finally decided to live, Port Lincoln, South Australia.

A couple of days short of her 70th birthday, Linda did indeed arrive in Sucre, Bolivia, South America. She celebrated her day with her beloved friends playing music. For three months she toured Chile, Bolivia and Argentina on a 125 Yamaha bought in Santiago and then sold 8,000 kms later in the same city, before flying out to visit her family in UK, friends in Europe and then returning to Australia.

Essentially traveling the world solo her entire life Linda's most important advice is to take a positive and open minded attitude, always trust your intuition, take things as they come and don't go looking for trouble.

Linda's deep love of folk music and motorcycling and her generous spirit reward her with many friends from many different parts of the world who always open their arms and homes to her.

"The motivation is travelling and meeting people. The motorcycle is the best way of doing that. I am not interested in records or going anywhere fast. Sponsorships are not worth it. For me, it's too much of a hassle. I want to do this trip slowly and go where I want. I have seen people who have to be at a certain place at a certain time for television. It really isn't worth it."

Linda believes that her independent spirit and positive attitude is a direct result of her upbringing by open minded and supportive parents. Her father insisted that "there is no such word as can't" and her mother, always a working wife, gave a strong example of a woman who, even in a loving relationship, made her own decisions in life and was an equal partner in the marriage. Linda was encouraged to be independent and, as long as her parents knew where she was and who she was with, she was not forbidden to go anywhere.

As age is taking its toll Linda has downsized her bike from the 250 to a 110 Honda 'postie' bike which she has kitted out with a big tank and is intending to use for touring in Australia when she has time between performing folk music and writing books.

All her books are available on Amazon in paperback or Kindle format.

Photos supplied by Linda Bootherstone-Bick

Tina on her beloved Ducati single.

10
TINA KARAN

AUSTRALIA'S FIRST AND ONLY WOMAN TO WIN AN AUSTRALIAN SPEEDWAY SIDECAR CHAMPIONSHIP

What is a Speedway Sidecar? A three-wheeled purpose built machine, housing a 1000cc motor and designed to only turn right at the end of the straight of an oval dirt track – that can be as short as 250 metres and up to 1600 metres. *"OH and no brakes with 2 people on board!"* Really there is no track or surface the same and the surface can change for each race on the same night. Tracks are generally flat or slightly banked and can be clay (not nice for bikes), shale, granite/sand, or dolomite. You just never know what you will be served up. One thing for sure is that it is superfast and full throttle from the time the tapes go up right to the checkered flag, about a minute and a half later, and speeds can reach around 250 kph. As the machines near the corners, they are mercilessly thrown sideways with the front wheel seemingly in opposite lock to the rear wheel, whilst experiencing strong centrifugal forces.

So, for the daring, Speedway is an exhilarating, adrenalin fuelled, crowd pleasing sport.

Tina Karan took to Speedway Sidecar racing "like a fish to water".

In the 1980s, whilst studying Fashion Design at Technical College, Tina became interested in fashion from earlier decades, in particular the Mod era of the 1960s. Her love of the styling and culture of the Mods of the UK led her as far as buying a Vespa scooter which she fashioned into period style, modifying with the additions of chrome, mirrors galore and foxtails. The scooter was her first experience on two-wheels but it was a short-lived relationship. In the years previous, Tina's older brother was quite regularly visited by his friend, Russell Mitchell who would roll up on his 900 Ducati Darmah. "I think that may have sown the seed a little without me realising". The scooter was soon traded for a Yamaha 400 and by that stage Tina and Russell had started dating. Tina mentions that one of their regular friends had a kaleidoscope of bikes and needed to sell a few and she perused the collection. The little yellow 1974 250 Desmo popped up and seemed to say 'you need to buy me' and it is a bike that Tina still owns and adores today.

Tina was 18 when her love affair with Speedway began. In 1985, Russell, working in Wickham, Western Australia, found out that he had a mate in Mt Newman, north west Western Australia, who had just started 'swinging' (a term used for a passenger) on a speedway sidecar. Tina was on holiday at the time in Melbourne, but Russell was keen to see their friend race. *"This triggered his competitive nature (he used to race Motocross but got too big) and said something to the effect "I reckon I can build something better than their bike and kick their arse" and away he went designing and constructing it. I thought it sounded pretty exciting too and not one to want to miss out on anything, claimed the passenger job."* Tina had never been to the speedway and had no idea what her self-appointed position entailed. She cut short her Melbourne holiday to head home and she and Russell headed off to the first meeting of the Claremont Speedway season to study the races and bikes. Witnessing the spectacle made her all the more excited about competing. There began Tina's illustrious career in Speedway Sidecar racing, one that spanned 27 years.

So what does a passenger do? *"The passenger is there to assist in the handling of the bike. In corners, we are down centimetres from the ground but we watch the front wheel to know where we should place our weight. Without a passenger the sidecar does not really get around corners well so our body position is crucial. This could be more forward or more back toward back wheel. Keeping the bike balanced is important on the start line too. They have a habit of tipping over due to the lean. Down the straights, we get our weight right back and over the back seat a little. This is to try to help get maximum drive. Sometimes we know where other riders are on the track and can* alert our rider with tap signals on their leg."

Russell built their race outfit around a Kawasaki 900cc, which they took to the abandoned and derelict Roebourne Speedway track to practice and develop their skills before hitting the big time at Claremont Speedway.

"When we appeared on the scene there were a few funny looks about how effective I would be, being 50 kg wringing wet. It didn't take long for the critics to agree that a lighter passenger was the way to go." (taken from Peter White's *100 More Aussie Legends of the Speedways*).

It didn't take long before the Tina and Russell's partnership form and racing prowess was awarding them positions on the podium and within 18 months they were rated second best in

Tina and Mark take out the Australian Sidecar Championship.

In the pits with Russell Mitchell at Claremont Speedway 1986.

Western Australia. In 1987 the Australian titles were held in Archerfield, Queensland and because the Western Australian state title was not taking place until after the Nationals, two riders had to be selected based only on their form. Tina and Russell were selected along with Dennis Nash (5 x Australian Sidecar Champion, 9 x WA Sidecar Champion and Motorcycling WA Hall of Fame Inductee). *"There we were, nobodies amongst some of the best riders in the country at an Australian Title."* With a 7th under their belt at the Nationals, then a 2nd in the WA State Titles, Tina and Russell were going from strength to strength, riding every event in the state that they could. However, in 1988 their partnership came to an end. Tina's skills as a passenger were highly sought after within the industry and it was not long before she was approached by Ed Blakney. Even though they enjoyed some success Tina didn't feel that they gelled as race partners. Mark Drew had not long entered the scene when Tina first witnessed his fast and smooth and impressive riding style on a Russell Mitchell built bike. The timing was fortuitous for both Tina and Mark as Tina still had her sights set on an Australian title and Mark was on the verge of losing his regular swinger. A month after their first meeting Mark contacted Tina to ask her if she would be interested in being his teammate.

"We hit the ground running, riding WA tracks and interstate events. The big Claremont circuit was my favourite, just that terminal speed at the end of those long straights. It was fantastic. Mark and I had a couple of really cracking seasons. 1992, 1993 and 1994 were full of successes, none more so than that magnificent Australian title win at Broken Hill. Yee-ha! I finally got it! And I'm still the only female to have won one." (taken from Peter White's *100 More Aussie Legends of the Speedway*). Up until around early 2000s, to be eligible to compete in the nerve racking Australian Title you must have won your state title or have placed 2nd. Rules then changed to only first placing in each state title, with other positions to qualify for available only to in-form riders. So, with only six state champions seeded, the qualifying event for the remaining 10 race positions is an incredible spectacle in itself.

The fastest speed that was recorded during Tina and Mark's time as a team came while racing the Aussie Long Track Title in Morgan (the event is the Morgan Mile). The local constabulary were there having a sticky beak and decided to see what the top speed was on the longest part of the track with their speed radar.

They dutifully approached Tina and Mark to advise that they reached close to 285 kmh. *"No brakes – who needs them!"*

Tina sustained quite a few injuries and broken bones over the years but there was one accident in 1988 that had Russell rattled and he didn't want her to continue. It was on the back straight at Claremont *"It was a handicap race and we were back on the 110 metre mark chasing down the back markers. A rider had troubles and he was out near the fence. He thought he could get to the infield before we came flying around pit corner. This was not the case and it ended up being a 3 or 4 bike pile up."* Tina had been knocked unconscious and was not breathing. She had to be revived on the track and only remembers waking up in hospital. She was back out on the track a few weeks later.

Another amazing event that Tina was involved with was of a different nature. Speedway on Ice! Without the proper spiked tyres that are used in Europe, competitors fashioned their own tyres by screwing in self-tappers. The great fun of the event was cut short by a few laps as the tyre screws had gouged the ice away and come precariously close to freezer pipework.

Tina and Mark's race partnership came to an end in 1996. The following years didn't quash Tina's competitive spirit, seeing her revel in water skiing, sky diving and inline hockey (hockey on roller blades) where her team won the bronze medal in the 1998 Australian Championships. Nor did these years quell her love of her beloved Ducati motorcycles. In Tina's stable resides her lovely little orange Ducati 250 single, a 1999 996 SPS, a 2000 996 SPS, and a 1994 Superlight.

Out of the blue in 2009, Tina received a phone call from her original race partner Russell Mitchell that returned her to the sport she loves. The offer – a return to Speedway Sidecar Racing but at the highest level imaginable – The World Titles to be held in La Reole, France. Tina hadn't thought much about Speedway for many years but the prospect of competing again was far too exciting to pass up. *"Off we went to a dry old local country track for some practice and setting up the bike. It all came back to us pretty quickly I have to say and off we went to France. La Reole was a long grass track so it was fast and we did well coming in fourth. Aussies dominated three of the top four placings. When we returned back to Perth we continued racing until 2011. We collected a couple of State titles* and competed in a couple of Aussie titles too. Blew an engine in one and finished about eighth in the other. Not very eventful. Still had fun. In 2011 we took part in a few meetings of the Sidecar grand slam that travels down the east coast, about 10 – 12 meetings in this event at different tracks. During the Mackay event on that tour, we hit a massive rut on ride line and it spat me off and Russell went over the bars but managed to stay on. Paul Pinfold nearly ran me over.

I couldn't continue, was a bit concussed and my left arm wasn't too good. I had tendon and soft tissue damage which took a while to come good. As I was moving to Qld in early 2012 and with my injury still repairing, it was not going to be possible to continue to race with a long distance partner so we again called it a day.

To be continued … you never know!!!

"Still have my trusty road bikes in the shed, so happy days."

Photos supplied by Tina Karan.

Tina and Mark Drew at the Wayville Showgrounds Speedway Spectacular, South Australia 1993.

Mandy aboard the bike on which she nearly lost her life.

11
MANDY BEALES

AUSTRALIA'S FIRST FEMALE SOLO MOTORCYCLE ROAD RACE CHAMPION

In 1999 Mandy Beales was 23 when she survived an horrific and unfathomable accident, but she did not let fear conquer her undying love of motorcycles. This event marked the beginning of a remarkable chapter in Mandy's life and a remarkable chapter in the history of motorcycle racing in Australia.

As a young woman, Mandy's striking face, form and skill behind the handlebars was well known within Adelaide's motorcycling communities. She was known as the chick on the blue bike (Kawasaki ZX9R Ninja) who could do wheelies and who smoked up the roads doing burn-outs. Mandy was a self-confessed "Rat Bag"! It was on this bike that Mandy almost met her maker!

"I had just finished work (as a cleaner) and I wanted to go for a ride. I wasn't speeding, I was just tired and, apparently, I fell asleep.

Mandy and one of her famous wheelies.

A taxi driver saw me slump over the petrol tank, I hit a tree and ended up with my kneecap ripped in half, I broke my left wrist, hand and arm, three ribs, snapped my scapula, lacerated my liver, bruised my pancreas and ruptured my spleen. I also had some skin missing and down one side of my body was black and blue. I remember waking up and there was blood splattered on the road in front of my face and I couldn't breathe. It was totally frightening." (interview with Mandy Beales, *The Advertiser* Magazine, Adelaide April 2009).

Coming from a lineage of rally car racing parents, the need for speed was in her blood but she also had the innate ability to race. Mandy's greatest inspiration is her mother, Lyn Peake, who was one of South Australia's first female jockeys, a winner at the Collingrove Hill Climb and now competes as a Master's Athlete 200 metre runner. Lyn was also the initiator of Mandy's lifetime connection with motorcycles when she bought her a Honda MR50 dirt bike. Being a 10-year-old country kid Mandy use to *"hoon around"* their farm but when they moved to suburbia, a few years later, the dirt bike was relegated to the shed. Thoughts of saving for a four-wheeled steed did not enter Mandy's mind. When she got a part-time job in a supermarket she saved furiously and as soon as she turned 16, got her licence and purchased a Honda CB250T. It was not long before Mandy determinedly saved again and when her unrestricted licence was issued she had her sights set on the very fast, very exciting, Kawasaki ZX9R Ninja.

Mandy's fascination with motorcycle racing developed whilst watching great racers like Mick Doohan on TV, but at that stage she did not know that a local race scene existed. This discovery only came after her death-defying misadventure when Shane Lynch of Adelaide Motorcycle Recovery, who had collected her crashed Ninja, recognised Mandy's potential for racing and also recommended that the race track may be a safer partner for Mandy and her motorcycle. It was with Shane's assistance that Mandy went to work in the pit crew of the local Ducati racing team of Jamie Videon and Russell Phillips. In three years she learnt a lot about the ins and outs of the inner workings of motorcycles and track techniques. In 2003, when she was 28, another life changing experience for Mandy occurred. Russell Phillips dragged his old Ducati TT2 out of his shed and allowed Mandy to have her very first ride, around the Mallala Motor Sport Park track. Yes, she was nervous and no, she didn't break any records, but it was in that very first lap that she knew what she wanted to do and that, of course, was race motorcycles.

Starting as a C-grader in the National Super Stock series in 2003, Mandy had sold her Ninja and her beloved electric guitar to purchase a race-suitable bike, being a Yamaha YZF-R6 600cc. With this purchase came a job offer from Yamaha World. The dealership realised the vastly growing market of women motorcyclists and knew that Mandy had the knowledge and savoir-faire the business needed. Mandy then went on to compete in the 2004 season of the Shell Advance Australian Superbike Championship (Super Stock and Super Sport) riding her 600cc and within 12 months was upgraded from C to B grade. At the time, Mandy had been quite happy to sit in C grade to develop her skills. However, in a possible attempt to oust Mandy from competition, an official accompanied by a lawyer, pushed for her to be up-graded early.

Mandy's race face.

Mandy in full flight.

They succeeded with the upgrade but must have turned on their heels when she went on to achieve more than even she could have imagined. The team at Kawasaki recognised Mandy's developing talent and offered her a factory-supported motorcycle. However, the acceptance of this deal meant Mandy had to give up her position at Yamaha World and she went on to work for Blackwell Funerals.

Mandy stared death in the face on more than one occasion. She broke the mould in every aspect of her life, working as a mortician, then funeral director for Blackwell Funerals (her major race sponsor) and racing motorcycles in what was a male dominated domain.

Going from strength to strength, Mandy was winning races and people were noticing.

With a burning desire to race in the 2006 125 Grand Prix series, Mandy's family and friends banded together and raised the funds to purchase the bike that she needed to compete, a Honda RS 125 GP. Mandy really hit her straps and accomplished her first major win, taking out the South Australian Championship 125 GP Series at Mallala Motor Sport Park South Australia.

A term quite often used in motorcycling especially when it comes to speed and handling is 'he rides like a girl'. Well, Mandy Beales put this term to bed!

Encountering a barrage of sexist attitudes on the track hardened her heart and made her more determined to succeed, but when overhearing a fellow racer say that she was just a "nice piece of arse" to follow around the track, she was heartbroken.

On many levels motorcycle racing is not for the faint of heart!

"As soon as you hit the tarmac, it's 'bang'! And you can't slow down and you can't back off, you are just there to go as fast as you can and develop the bike's performance. You take a corner and your knee is on the ground, and when you hit the brakes you're screaming 'shit' in your helmet, 'cos you think you're not going to stop, but somehow you end up stopping and pulling it together. If you're not out of your seat thinking, 'I'm not going to be able to stop', then you're not going fast enough. The moment you cross the finish line, whether you're first or 20th, it's like, 'wow, I've done it'." (interview with Mandy Beales, *The Advertiser* Magazine, Adelaide April 2009).

Mandy with some of her many trophies.

The reality of the expense of racing was hard to swallow. Even with factory support (meaning the loan of a motorcycle and discounted parts), meeting the constant expense of airfares and accommodation, race entry fees and forking out thousands per meet for tyres alone was too taxing for Mandy to continue. So in 2007, Mandy sold her beloved Honda RS 125 GP and repaid her family and friends. It was the first time in Mandy's 31 years that she was bikeless!

Jerry Kooistra had been keeping a keen eye on Australia's finest talent and one name kept coming to the fore, Mandy Beales. As one of Australia's premier motorcycle builders, Jerry knew he had to have someone very special to ride his renowned and very valuable Honda 'twins' 350cc and 500cc, to succeed the legendary Bill Horsman (nine times Australian champion and Isle of Man TT winner) when he retired. Jerry, like other bike builders/owners knew, you want your bike to win but you don't want your bike to get 'binned'! He needed a racer who understood his bikes, understood the magnitude of the experience, also a racer who had unbridled talent.

In the first lap of Mandy's first race at Mallala aboard the 350cc Honda special, she broke Bill Horsman's lap record.

Pre-race preparation was paramount to Mandy's mindset. She would not only draw the race track on a piece of A4 paper, but she would also note down the optimum gear change and brake application positions and the bumps and turns that may bring her unstuck. She would study this intensely and visualise herself riding the perfect lap over and over again, and she would never go out on the track without her lucky odd socks (one green and one white).

Mandy with the legendary Jeremy Burgess.

Was this the secret to her success?

In October of 2007, Mandy won her first prize money at the Australian Motorcycle Grand Prix at Phillip Island, in the Australian Superbikes Races to the tune of $25.00 – a token sum that represented so much to Mandy that she never wanted to cash the cheque.

In the lead up to the 2008 National Classic Titles, Mandy won 31 of the 34 races in which she rode.

"Mortician wants to bury opposition at Barbagello", a headline that would send shivers up the spine of any opposition rider, was published by *The West Australian* newspaper on Sunday 16 November 2008, only giving them a few days to steel themselves against the rider

Signing autographs for her young fans.

some called "The Undertaker". Mandy arrived in Western Australia as the front runner for the Championship Title, riding against names such as Dave Cole (New Zealand), the defending champion, and Brendan Roberts, the Ducati Superstock pilot.

At Barbagello Mandy did indeed take out the top prize in the Period 3 (350cc) Classic becoming **the first female to ever win an Australian solo Road Racing Championship.**

Mandy gracefully bowed out of motorcycle racing due to unfortunate health issues, but still to date, the mention of her name brings forth exuberance from avid and adoring members of Australia's motorcycling fraternity who not only appreciate her innate talent but also recognise the sincere, beautiful spirit that resides within Mandy Beales.

Mandy Beales is a true icon.

Mandy will ride again! Her wounds will heal and Australia will be fortunate to again see her striking face, form and skill behind a set of handlebars of her choice.

"To ride fast, you have to ride smooth, so forget about going fast, ride smoothly and the speed will come."

Photos supplied by Mandy Beales.

The World's Fastest Woman on a motorcycle.

12

KIM KREBS

THE WORLD'S FASTEST WOMAN ON A MOTORCYCLE

Being awarded the coveted Red Hat and welcomed into the fold of the International 200 mph (mile per hour) Club does not come easy! To be eligible to don the Red Hat the competitor must exceed 200 mph (321.86 kph) whilst setting a record for the vehicle's class. More women have been to outer space than wear the 200 Club's Red Hat for motorcycle land speed achievements!

Kim Krebs races motorcycles on the Earth's rare salt lakes. She pushes the boundaries of speed that would test only the bravest of souls! She is exceptional, she doesn't seek praise, approval or recognition and when interviewed she so very fluently proses the 'whys' of her passion and how she achieves these accolades!

"As they say ... if it was easy, everyone would be doing it!"

Land speed racing is considered the ultimate pursuit of achieving maximum possible speeds without launching off the ground. It typically involves a 5 km 'run up' then your average speed is recorded over the next mile (1.6 km). Records are established from a two-way average pass, up and down the track. It's not as easy as it sounds, as one of the biggest hurdles is the almost complete lack of traction. *"It's like riding on a hard packed dirt road with a gravel surface. You are skating and wheel spinning constantly. The faster you go, the more unstable your handling gets, as your machine literally becomes flighty (a Boeing 747 takes off at 180 mph)."* Reaching 200 mph (321.86 kph) on the ground is difficult, doing it with limited traction is even harder. Going at speeds way beyond, while seated on a 'sit-on' bike is exponentially more difficult.

Kim was only six years old when she first encountered a motorcycle. Her uncle, a farm mechanic, regularly serviced a fleet of monkey bikes that were part of the act for a nearby circus. Whilst Kim was visiting one day, her uncle gave her and her cousins the chance to ride them around a back paddock of his property. *"I still remember barrelling down the paddock, heading straight for the fence and have remembered ever since, which way to turn the throttle."*

By the age of 10, Kim and her cousins were hooked! They had all bought dirt bikes, Kim's was a Honda XR75cc, *"and the rest is history".*

Growing up on acreage Kim had quite a good practice circuit *"for my childhood imagination".* In support, Kim's dad purchased a bike to ride along with her when they would go on family outings, camping and riding through farms and forests. This family fun lasted for a few years until *"all the Dads decided that sailing was their next adventure. I was the only one of all my cousins who kept on with the bikes."*

At 16, Kim's passion for motorcycles had only grown. She had saved her pennies to buy her first road bike and hoped for approval from her parents that would seal the deal. Years later her mother still found the notes that Kim had scattered around their house and buried deep within the linen cupboards, asking *"Is it ok? You don't mind if I get a motorbike?"*

Kim Krebs.

Knowing that she could achieve her motorcycle licence at 16 years and nine months, she convinced her uncle to test ride her desired Kawasaki GPZ600.

The Kawasaki was special to Kim. She had

watched and admired an inspirational neighbour, who had gone from never having ridden a bike to purchasing and loving a GPZ600 and Kim decided to follow in her footsteps. Kim had saved up the money for her GPZ600 (1984 model) from part-time jobs and bought it secondhand in 1988 with 35,000 km on the clock. By the time she upgraded to a Yamaha FJR1100, another 100,000 kms had passed under its wheels. By the way, Kim's first 4-wheeled purchase came only when she reached the age of 42, in the form of a utility so that she could transport her race bike.

In the late 80s Kim was a university student on a shoestring budget, so whenever her bike needed servicing, or the registration was due, she reduced her spending and madly saved the money needed. *"I remember being really short of cash one year, having reduced my weekly allocation of money for food down to $3.50 a week. Enough to buy a loaf of bread and a bag of oranges."*

Kim had her first taste of motorcycle racing when she joined the Pine Gully Racing Association and participated in an InterVarsity (University) Road Race track days. It was several years later in 2005 that she took up historic road racing. The attraction of race events, like the MotoGP and World Superbikes at Phillip Island was where Kim met and befriended many like-minded motorcycling enthusiasts. This is where Kim met Greg Watters! Greg is Australia's most accomplished motorcycle land speed racer and has a lifelong connection to motorsports. Racing and having been a V8 racing team mechanic in many different events (drag racing, track days, V8 Ute road racing series etc.), he is proficient in the intricacies of race mechanics. So, when Greg offered Kim the opportunity to go land speed racing she said *"yes"*, then asked him what it was!

With the philosophy *"Try before you say no!"*, Kim was racing with Greg only five months after what became a life changing offer.

There is no way to practice Land Speed Racing, although Kim did ask the local policeman in her one-cop town of Yackandandah, his reply was *"No Way!"*

With only one event per year at Lake Gairdner, South Australia, Kim and Greg soon looked to the iconic speed trials on Lake Bonneville in Utah, USA.

Their philosophy is that the only way to approach any event is to make sure the bike is prepared and treat every run like it's the only opportunity you'll ever have.

In her first attempt on the salt at Lake Gairdner in 2006, riding a 1996 Suzuki GSXR750, Kim achieved an impressive 166 mph (267 kph). Kim's first thoughts were **"I can go so much faster!"** In the same year Kim and Greg met Californian fireman Jim Higgins and they hit it off. Jim had travelled into the heart of South Australia's desert country, to Lake Gairdner, for the Dry Lake Racers Annual Speed Week, to race his Buell turbocharged-nitrous motorcycle. Jim's bike sustained damage to its engine early in the race week, so he had time up his sleeve to mingle with his fellow competitors. Kim, Greg and Jim formed a strong bond and from this meeting of like minds, 'Black Art Racing' was born. When deciding on a team name, the three team mates all acknowledged that it is most certainly a 'black art' to create a bike with so much power.

The next two years saw Lake Gairdner washed out, with unseasonal late summer rain. But in 2009, Kim rose to the challenge again and achieved the celebrated title of Australia's Fastest Woman on a motorcycle. Kim set a Land Speed Record achieving 188.41 mph (303 kph) at Lake Gairdner on a turbocharged Suzuki GSXR750. Later, in the same year she joined Greg and Jim at Bonneville Salt Flats in Utah with the three riders sharing the turbocharged 1996 Suzuki GSX1350R Hayabusa (Japanese for 'Peregrine falcon', a bird that often serves as a metaphor for speed). As well as what was to become the slightly famous eBay purchase, a sight-unseen 1999 Suzuki GSXR750. It was on board this 750cc bike that Kim and the team went on to set multiple American land speed records.

Lake Gairdner, South Australia and Bonneville Salt Flats, Utah USA, are two totally different landscapes, but both are incredibly beautiful and serene! Lake Gairdner is positioned approximately 90 metres above sea level and Bonneville approximately 1600 metres. Lake Gairdner is a natural lake, whereas Bonneville is an ancient landscape that has become modified from potash mining that sees the natural salts extracted from the system between each winter and summer. There is also a huge difference in air thickness between the two sites, which makes faster speeds much more achievable in the thinner air of the 'States'.

Black Art Racing – Greg (left), Kim and Jim (right).

So what goes through Kim's mind when attempting a Land Speed Record? *"7 gears! I have had a few fast runs where I only got into 5th gear. So I try and remember to count gears and make sure I have at least 2 goes at 6th, to make sure I'm in top gear. I have complete confidence in my race partners, as they do in me, so I never have any doubts about the bike and what we've done to it. I climb on, relax and focus on going hard in through each gear. The turbo only kicks in at around 10,000 rpm and redlines at 13,000 rpm, so I need to do all my gear changes around 11–12,000 rpm. Staying relaxed on the bike, while finding the most aero-dynamic position and counting the measured mile markers as they flash by. You wouldn't think that it's hard to count to 6 (to measure the gears) and 3 (to know when I'm about to enter the measured mile) at the same time, but sometimes I forget both numbers and have been known to go through the 5 mile, still at full throttle, with rescue chasing, thinking that something has gone wrong, like a jammed throttle."*

In the summer of 2014, untameable fires ravaged Victoria. One particular fire decimated every inch of the ground and tore through Greg's home farm. The devastation for Greg and his family who had battled the raging flames, spread through not only his home and his farming enterprise, but melted his and 'Black Art Racing's' beloved bikes. It melted the dyno machine, the workshop and every other part that composed the wonderful machines that set the team free on the salt. Undeterred Greg, Kim and Jim picked up the pieces and soldiered on.

Up until the destructive fires of 2014, Kim and Greg would ship their two bikes to the USA. A voyage that required two months and more money than they actually had. The fire was a turning point for the team.

"We pooled our resources and, adding to our 'eBay 750', bought a US based Hayabusa." Not having to ship the bikes each year meant a great saving, of both time and money for the team.

There was no racing in 2014, but by February 2015, Kim and Greg again returned to the salt flats of Lake Gairdner. Like the phoenix rising from the ashes, it was time to test the new bikes. Lost was all the aerodynamic development and mechanical ingenuity of the proven bikes, but what emerged were two fast machines. By the end of the speed trial, Kim had ridden the 750 to 212 mph (341.18 kph). Owing to the relative air density, compared to the high altitudes of Bonneville, this was the equivalent to 230 mph (370.14 kph) in the States. 'Black Art Racing' now knew they had created another stable of fast, record breaking machines.

Land Speed Racing isn't for the faint-hearted, the impatient or the reckless. Kim's attempts always start with the sound of her own heart beating. With *"5 kilometres run up to speed, 3 kilometres flat-chat, and 3 kilometres to slow down",* Kim treats every run as the only one she is going to get.

"Going this fast, everything slows down and I feel like I'm in a zone where there are literally more moments in time to make decisions. The decisions that my life may depend on!"

The 2016 season got off to a flying start for Kim, again breaking a land speed record at the Dry Lake Racer's Speed Week topping 212 mph (342.27 kph) on the Suzuki 750cc. This was the first time that Kim went over 200 mph in the Southern Hemisphere, although it had long become the norm for her in her Northern Hemisphere racing campaigns. Kim broke the existing Australian record by an astounding 42.50 mph (68.40 kph).Again she was celebrated and awarded with the Australian equivalent of the Red Hat, membership to the DRLA 200 Club.

In September of 2016, Kim, Greg and Jim took their fleet of now three bikes to the Bonneville Motorcycle Speed Trials. The 750, the 'Big Busa', and their new turbo 600. Kim qualified on the 750 at 220 mph(354 kph) on her own 2009 record of 209 mph (336.35 kph), but the bike sustained engine damage on the return run. Next on the Hayabusa, she topped 244 mph (394.28 kph) and set a record at 241 mph (387.85 kph). At the meet Greg was the fastest rider on a 'sit-on bike' and Kim was the fastest female. 'Black Art Racing's' next stop was The Colorado Mile, a 1 Mile Top Speed Racing event held at Front Range Airport. Participants show what they've got on a one mile straight, with a half-mile shut down. They compete to be the best of the best for outright top speed, no classes, to try and set a record in Colorado and a chance to earn their spot in a MPH+ Club!

The slogan is ***"3 Days–1 Mile–No Speed Limit"***

Kim climbed aboard the 600 and achieved a 178 mph (286 kph) pass, next up was the Hayabusa. *"My first pass on the Busa was going well until 4th gear when it shuddered and the oil light come on — it had spat out a rod!!!"* By the end of the meet all three bikes sustained damage, but Black Art Racing showed that they had created a 200 mph capable 600cc motorcycle.

Kim Krebs at top speed.

Black Art Racing had, in 2015, already unsettled the Colorado locals with Greg's prowess in race mechanics seeing competitors on four wheels pulling 'all nighters' to retune their vehicles in desperate attempts to surpass Black Art Racing and their two wheeled mega speed machines. Kim topped 207 mph (333.13 kph) and Greg 237 mph (381.41 kph). Only one Nissan GTR managed to creep past Greg at 242 mph (389.46 kph), that was with four wheels, five times the horse power and four disc brakes for stopping. A far cry from the bikes that were set up for a gentle slowing over two miles.

Land speed racing records are chased by only a few passionate and committed people. It is a sport that seeks to find out who you are, what you are capable of, and therefore, how fast you can make your machine

The harsh salt surface.

go. You do this for almost no recognition. In fact, every incredible run, every personal achievement is rewarded only with the equivalent of a shopping docket; a print out of your speed, the relative air density and the prevailing wind speed and direction. The only proof you have that you went as fast as you could.

So what's next for Kim Krebs? *"I'm always open to finding out. I love bikes. I love racing and I'm very fortunate to have two racing partners in Jim and Greg, where we all get along so well, and combined we are an extremely successful bunch of amateurs with a swag of Australian, American and World records under our belts."*

At the close of the 2016 racing season, Kim Krebs earned the wonderful title of the Fastest Woman in the world on a 'sit-on' motorcycle. Kim achieved a monumental 244 mph (392.68 kph) surpassing Leslie Portfield's 2007 effort of 241 mph (387.85 kph) on a one-way pass.

"Land Speed Racing is all about trying to get the most out of yourself and your machine and finding the limits for both."

SOME OTHER ACHIEVEMENTS WORTH NOTING:

* First ever attempt at LSR was 166 mph record for a 750cc in Australia
* 2009 was the first time ever that an Australian woman went over 200 mph
* 2016 was the first time an Australian woman went over 200 mph in Australia top speed of 244 mph – the fastest any woman has ever gone on a 'sit-on' motorcycle (excluding the amazing achievements of Eva Hakansson and Valerie Thompson in streamliners)
* 2011 recipient of the USA SheMotoLandSpeed Achievers Award (for non American recipient)
* 2012 Motorcycling Australia's Rider's Division Motorcyclist of the Year
* 2010 led the Barry Sheane tribute ride to the MotoGP
* 2013 featured in a Nurofen advert that has screened around the world
* A regular motivational speaker to schools, community groups and business, to help them recognise the hidden talents that might exist within

Photos supplied by Dominik Seidlecki and Kim Krebs

Launching the Kawasaki ZX-14.

13
KELLIE BUCKLEY

AUSTRALIA'S PREMIER MOTORCYCLE JOURNALIST

At the age of 23, Kellie Buckley became the first woman in Australia to become the News Editor of a major motorcycling magazine, 'Australia Motorcycle News'. Kellie knows motorcycles. She knows the culture.

Growing up in Mudgee, regional New South Wales, Kellie spent *"far too many afternoons at the local motorcycle dealer sitting on the brand-new Yamaha PW (pee-wee) 50"* that was parked out the front. Rocking back and forth on the centre-stand, and pretending she was actually riding, Kellie imagined herself pulling out onto the street and riding it around to her Nan's house to show it off, rehearsing in her mind what she'd say when she got there.

Most teenagers of the day had posters of rock stars on their wall, but not Kellie, she had posters of motorcycles, always nagging her parents to visit friends whose kids had motorbikes so she could

Kellie Buckley.

have a ride. Kellie's father was no stranger to motorcycling, owning an old Harley-Davidson shovel head which *"he spent far too much time and money customising with countless front ends, a myriad of paint schemes, and even going so far as fitting fuel injection and a power commander – pioneering stuff in the early 1990s".*

Thankfully Kellie's father, recognised the flame that resides within Kellie's spirit and this flame was not going to subside. Realising it was more than just a passing phase, he arrived home late one night with a bright red Suzuki DES 80 tied to the back of his truck.

"I think it was my first true love."

Kellie would ride every chance she could get, spending hours and hours riding around and around the small area her father had fenced off in their yard which was only big enough that she could just and briefly snick second gear. It was this bike that got her hooked on the smell of two-stroke and it was then that she realised the intricacy and detail of riding and learned to appreciate the inner workings of a motorcycle. *"One which infuriated my mother that I could love and care for something so much while I had "a bedroom that looks like that!"."*

A couple of years later Kellie's dad bought her a near-new Honda XR100, a more reliable bike. This meant he was more willing to take her to places where she could practice clutch, throttle and brake control. Unbeknown to her at the time the time spent *"just doing doughnuts"* in her parent's yard, creating elaborate designs in the gravel, passing hours, trying to figure out how to keep the front wheel aloft, made Kellie an accomplished rider. Kellie was nine years old.

"Other days I'd pretend I was lining up for races, heart pounding, and letting my nine-year-old imagination stand me on podiums with great applause until my brother appeared to tell me it was time for dinner. I'd sneak into the local newsagent and got yelled at by old Arthur for hiding behind the newsstands and reading Australasian Dirt Bike Magazine. When I saw a shooting star, or on birthdays, I'd always wish one day I'd be able to race the International Six Day Enduro. Adults would ask me what I wanted to be when I grow up and I'd answer," a postman! So I can ride motorbikes all day."

Before Kellie turned 10, motorcycles were her life.

Kellie and dad on his Shovelhead, circa 1987.

Kellie's dad was always mad about motorcycles, and he still is. Her brother had a late 1970s Yamaha DT 175, the two-stroke six speed, and Kellie spent her next few teenage years discovering how to kick start the bike, standing on a couple of old fuel drums for assistance. After completing boarding school at the age of 20, she moved to Newcastle, NSW, and needed to find a job. With an undying persistence and determination, Kellie walked into every motorcycle dealership in the local area to ask if there was a position available. Finally, Chris Hirst from Kawasaki Newcastle agreed to give her a go. *"Accessories and spare parts became my world and there wasn't a part number for an early – model KX oil seal or gasket that I didn't know off by heart."*

At the end of 2001, Kellie learnt motorcycling's toughest lesson. Her dad was contracted to cart cotton in the tiny northern NSW town of Croppa Creek. He had called asking for her help, needing someone to drive the harvester for a couple of weeks. In the mid-summer's searing heat, with no hesitation Kellie packed up her Yamaha TRX 850 and rode the 600 km northwest to meet him. Kellie's dad owned an impressive Cagiva Raptor 1000cc. He needed help! Kellie's father knew that she had the riding skill to deliver the earnings from the business to Moree (66 kms) to cash the cheque. *"Take my bike if you like"* he offered. She loved the power of the Raptor's TL 1000 Suzuki donor engine. The only hiccup was being unfamiliar with the weight and the characteristics of an upright naked bike. After making arrangements to meet her Dad at the Croppa Creek Pub a couple of hours later, Kellie set off! With temperatures well above 40°C and the pub *'just down the road'*, she removed her jacket and gloves and tied them to the back seat.

"At a fair clip I hit a pothole, which tore the bars out from my hands and spat me off the bike. Once I stop rag-dolling down the God-knows-how-hot asphalt, my shredded body burning from being torn apart by hot, coarse bitumen.

All I could do was jump to my feet and run around in circles to try and think about something other than the pain. The bike had cartwheeled itself into pieces and lay in the centre of the road and after I squinted up and down the long, flat and frightfully remote road, I looked down at my body and realised the magnitude of the damage. I'd skinned myself. Both hands were a bloodied mess of torn flesh, my exposed palms the first thing to hit the ground at 100 and something kays an hour. The rest of me, not much better. Something, I still don't know what, managed to pierce my kneecap, I'd ground the corner of my hipbone, my stomach, shoulders, forearms and thighs all skinless and stinging in the searing heat."

An unlikely saviour appeared, an old bloke in an old white ute, he sang out *"get in, I'll take you into Moree Hospital, but if I go over 80 K's an hour she will overheat, okay?".* It took her a long time to realise that she still wasn't bleeding. When she looked down into the foot-well of the ute she realised the centimetre of clear fluid her Blundstones were sitting in had seeped from her wounds. She went into shock!

Kellie only rides without a jacket on very rare occasions and has never and will never ride without gloves again.

Kellie's love of motorcycling never wavered.

Laying her employment foundations at the Kawasaki dealership, she spent a lot of time talking to importers and built a firm relationship with the team at Monza Imports, a private business that distributes some of the world's leading motorcycle brands. When a phone-sales position became available at its Sydney-based warehouse she jumped at the opportunity. *"A great place to work, a fun and relaxed environment where every single employee was there because of the deep love of motorcycles made for some enormously fond memories. But four or five years in I was craving another challenge, so I had a quiet word with*

Kellie on Honda Z50R, circa 1984.

the universe to keep an eye out for one for me."

It was now that Kellie's love of motorcycles expanded into a love of racing. The 400 cc road racing class, which at the time was booming in popularity on the East Coast, enticed Kellie to the track. Riding a Honda VFR400, she began racing, achieving varying levels of success. Her wish to the universe was just about to materialise. Taking a day off work she booked herself into a quiet, mid-week track day to spend some time on her bike before the next race.

"The day was going well. The sun was shining, I had the entire garage to myself, and Dad and I were making inroads with the set-up. That was until, at about 11 AM all these blokes wearing brand-new gear rolled in, all on brand-new bikes and, knowing the ego is generally associated with the situation, Dad and I looked at each other with an all-knowing eye roll and I prepared myself for the belittling which was sure to ensue." When helmets were removed the legendary road racers and media faces that she had only ever read about in Australian Motorcycle News stood before her; Kenny Wootton, Mick Matheson, Matt Shields and Greg Reynolds. Kellie was star-struck!

She went about her normal day until she plucked up the courage to initiate a conversation. By the end of the day, Kellie and her Dad were having a beer with Matt Shields (a freelance journalist who has had the role of Editor for magazines including 'Australian Motorcycle News', 'Australasian Dirt Bike' magazine, and 'Australian Mountain Bike' magazine). *"By the end of my second schooner I was listening to myself talking up the advantages of having a female staff member on the country's best motorcycle magazine."*

Even though Kellie awoke the next morning scolding herself for being so bold, a few hours later while answering the phone at Monza her boldness paid off! Mick Matheson (Editor at 'Australian Road Rider', and Video Producer at 'Phantom 2 Media') was on the other end of the line asking whether Kellie was serious when she said she'd like to work for 'Australian Motorcycle News'.

Starting as a staff journalist for 'Australian Motorcycle News' in May 2006, Kellie worked for seven years, alongside three editors and worked her way through every role (except art director).

"I was appointed the highest rank in Australian motorcycle journalism. Becoming the editor of AMCN was a

goal I'd set myself very early on and, like my first job in bikes at Kawasaki Newcastle, it was sheer persistence and determination that got me there."

Kellie achieved the title of the first woman in Australia to be appointed as the editor of the country's highest selling car or motorcycle magazine.

"I had my knockers, always the blokes with the biggest egos who were slower than me, of course. No different, I suspect, to what my male counterparts copped. By and large I had enormous support and acceptance by everyone in the industry. That is not to say I didn't need to prove myself time and time again, I did and I understand and respect the reasons why. In both Australian and world launches I had to ride harder than everyone else to earn my place, but I understood it and I did it. I knew I needed to earn respect from readers, too. After all, I started off an avid AMCN reader and if a woman wanted to become the editor of my favourite magazine, I damn well would have made sure she deserved to be there, too."

On 9 February 2010, Kellie was chosen amongst six journalists from some of Australia's leading motorcycle magazines to launch the latest 'brute-force' motorcycle, at Victoria's Heathcote Park dragstrip. Triumph launched its 367 kg 2300cc Rocket III Roadster, and Kellie conquered it. Kellie beat every Aussie journalist in a 'Chicago Shootout' drag race, taking out the trophy with an impressive 12.14 second pass. In 2012, she took the dragstrip again on a Kawasaki ZX-14R, this was the world's fastest accelerating production motorcycle.

Kellie made a conscious decision to rarely mention her gender when writing motorcycle test reviews. She wanted to work for *Australian Motorcycle News* for exactly the same reason everyone else did, because she loved bikes. *"I worked very hard to earn my place in the industry and to make quite sure I wasn't merely there as the token girl. Readers came to respect my work and my opinion and I'm sincerely grateful how welcoming each and every reader was when I finally took over the top job in 2013. In fact, it took two years in the editor's chair before I received my first and only gender-specific hate mail from a reader in my entire nine years. So I printed it word for word and was showered in phone calls and letters of support from the readers, which was unexpected and very, very moving.* Australian Motorcycle News *gave me some amazing once-in-a-lifetime opportunities.*

Opportunities I'll never forget. I've ridden KTMs in Austria, Suzukis in Las Vegas, Can-Ams in Canada, BMWs in Spain, Harleys in Tokyo. I've peered wide-eyed through hedges on the Isle of Man, stood trackside at the Pikes Peak International Hill Climb. I've shared a beer with Jeremy Burgess, Miguel Galuzzi, and Giacomo Agostioni. I've ridden hundreds of different motorcycles, most of them brand spankers and some being one of just a handful of people in the world to do so. Sure, I've crashed more bikes than most people will probably ride in their lives, but no one can ever accuse me of not having a bloody good go. Though it wasn't all wheelies and glamour. AMCN was, and will probably be, the hardest thing I've ever done. The energy needed to produce 148 pages of high quality content every two weeks for my nigh-on 10 years is enormous. I'm enormously proud of what I achieved during my time at AMCN."

Kellie resigned from 'Australian Motorcycle News' at the end of 2015, with 231 editions under her belt.

As at 2016, Kellie is still doing what she loves most in the world, riding motorbikes, testing them, and writing about them.

Photos supplied by Kellie Buckley and *Australian Motorcycle News*.

Competing in Adventure Trials on the Gold Coast.

Mad Meg's winning smile.

14
MEGHAN 'MAD MEG' RUTLEDGE

WINNER OF BACK TO BACK AUSTRALIAN WOMEN'S SUPERCROSS CHAMPIONSHIPS & AUSTRALIA'S PREMIER FEMALE MOTOCROSS RIDER

'Smooth, Hard and Fast' is Meghan 'Mad Meg' Rutledge's motto, and a motto that she lives by.

At the age of 4 Meghan well and truly hit the ground running when she first climbed aboard a dirt bike in 1999. Her two older sisters were already racing and Meghan was determined to join in the fun. In between the ages of 4 and 9 she rapidly developed her skills to the point of winning the 2004 NSW State Motocross titles against a grid of boys on 65cc motorbikes. It was this win that ignited her passion for racing motorcycles on dirt. By the age of 14 she had won three Junior Australian Motocross Championships. Meghan learnt at a very early age that if you ride smooth and train hard you will be fast!

Under the guidance, training and watchful eye of Australia's premier Motocross coach and founder of the Moss Institute, Greg Moss, Meg was welcomed into his fold and flourished. Greg's twin boys Matt and Jake Moss (two of Australia's premier champion

Race preparation.

Mad Meg airborne.

motocross riders) are Meghan's heroes. She professes that they have always encouraged her to follow her dreams. *"I have been coaching for 30 years and only occasionally do I find the perfect combination – A smile every time they ride the bike, a good stance on the bike and total respect for their parents. Meg exceeds at all three, so improving every ride was a no brainer." Greg Moss*

And so, began Meghan's domination of her sport!

In 2008, Motorcycling Australia held its Inaugural Australian Championship for Junior females. Meghan claimed the title. At the time Meghan worked tirelessly as a lifeguard and saved every cent so that she could afford to compete overseas.

In 2010, amongst a swag of motocross wins, Meghan became a grant recipient from Layne Beachley's Aim for the Stars Foundation, Australia's leading Foundation inspiring and empowering girls and women to achieve their goals. This gave Meghan a boost as it meant valued monetary support to help her continue and improve within her beloved sport.

In 2011 the accolades continued with, at the age of 16, 'Mad Meg' being nominated for Female Sportsperson of the year in The Deadly Awards, which recognises the contributions of Aboriginal and Torres Strait Islanders to their community and to Australian Society.

Meghan certainly possesses star quality! She is in constant demand by the media for interviews, was featured in a 2012 episode on ABC3 – 'The 3 Factor', which presented up and coming Australian kids aged 10 – 16 years who excel in their chosen field and who are inspiring and aspirational. Meghan, certainly fits the bill.

In the same year, when Meghan turned 17, she was crowned the Queen of Geneva Supercross Champion and became the Australian Women's Motocross champion to boot.

The understanding of the complexities of the sport of motocross and supercross is only fully realized by competitors. To the lay person, watching Meghan 'Mad Meg' Rutledge sliding and powering through powdered dirt tracks via YouTube, it is hard to fathom the mental and physical intensity, the riding skill and the focus that is so apparently needed to succeed.

Success after success after success came for Meghan, gloriously taking out the 2011 and 2012 (at the age of 18) Australian Women's Motocross Championship Title, then finishing the 2013 and 2014 FIM Women's World Motocross Championship in 2nd place, clocking the fastest lap time in most races.

Meghan travelled to Phillip Island in 2013 to compete against a field of world class riders in the 2013 Eve Sports Australian Women's Supercross Championships. Three intense rounds saw Meghan aboard her Kawasaki KX250F against the USA's two fastest racers. Meghan won and took the crown!

When a competitor achieves so many titles in a short period of years it becomes monumental and overwhelming to document every award and every title in one condensed chapter. Without a doubt this applies to the incredibly skilled Meghan 'Mad Meg' Rutledge.

Kawasaki Australia has notably been supportive and encouraging to up and coming motorcycling talent in Australia. Meghan's incredible drive, talent and determination did not go unnoticed and Kawasaki Australia awarded her their support. Meghan recognises that without the support of Kawasaki and their incredible machines, she could not be achievingthe dreams that she is now living.

The tug of war between time and location competing across the globe, racing in both Australia and internationally at the FIM Women's World Motocross Championship events, is taxing.

"Anybody who knows me understands that I am always chasing a challenge."

Meghan's entry into the competition of 2015 came to a screaming halt when she sustained a severe thumb injury. This came on top of a fractured ankle in early 2014. True to form, injury did not hold her back. Meghan made the most of her time out from motocross and diversified by keeping and improving her fitness and motor skills with the purchase of a Kawasaki Jet Ski and continued her regular training at the gym every weekday, swimming and still riding every weekend. Even under the grip of injury Meghan's focus did not waiver.

In June of 2016 'Mad Meg' rose to the occasion again when on top of competing in the Australian and world Motocross championships, she grabbed The Tatts Finke Desert Race by the horns. The Finke is Australia's most difficult off road, multi terrain, two day race with riders tackling approximately 450 kilometres, racing

Meghan 'Mad Meg' Rutledge.

throughout one of the world's most remote regions. It tests the stamina and endurance of the planet's most skilled and mentally and physically fit riders. Wrangling a bout of the flu, and the extreme desert conditions Meghan never faltered. With the throttle wide open, Meghan pushed herself and her Kawasaki KX250F to the limits.

Of 409 registered competitors Meghan placed 6th in her class and 29th overall.

What does the future hold for Meghan Rutledge?

The inspirational and aspirational Meghan 'Mad Meg' Rutledge, generously makes time in her intense schedule holding coaching schools for juniors in the art of riding and racing in which she so clearly excels.

Meghan 'Mad Meg' Rutledge's story of success is to be continued …

Photos supplied by Kawasaki Australia

15

TANIA LAWRENCE

THE FIRST FEMALE PRESIDENT OF MOTORCYCLING AUSTRALIA

Being elected to preside over a national organisation whose intricacies comprise managing a multitude of disciplines in the sport of motorcycling, a complexity of safety issues and a membership of insatiable devotees to the sport, takes a steely but flexible persona. Fortunately, Tania Lawrence is an avid and accomplished motorcyclist and a successful business woman, and proved she was up to the task.

Tania was elected as President of Motorcycling Australia in 2015 and became the first Western Australian and the first woman to be appointed to the role. This was no small feat, as the organisation manages more than 32,700 competitors, 350 + affiliated clubs and over 3000 registered officials. Subsequent to this appointment, she was elected as the President of FIM Oceania representing Australia and New Zealand, which resulted in a seat on the Board of the International Motorcycling Federation (FIM) in Geneva. Tania's devotion and commitment to motorcycling is clear as her roles on both boards were on a voluntary basis.

At the time of her appointment, Tania was, and still is, employed by Australia's largest independent oil and gas company, Woodside Energy Ltd., where she is responsible for optimising Woodside's international growth and performance. With over 16 years' of senior level experience in strategy, risk and governance, a Bachelor of Economics and a Bachelor of Arts (Honours) degree, Tania was certainly a sound and wise choice for both of her positions.

Tania Lawrence.

During her tenure as President, Tania worked with Motorcycling Australia and the FIM, to improve the position of Australian competitive motorcyclists on the worldwide stage.

"Joining the MA Board and FIM Board as the Oceania representative was such a highlight for me. I am very proud of what our Board delivered in such a short time, especially with re-establishing our reputation on the international stage and restoring the financial stability and credibility with the national body. The groundwork is now also laid to create a national unified approach to grow the sport and advocate strongly for the interests of motorcyclists."

Tania has, to date, been riding for 25 years competitively and recreationally, both on road and off-road. *"I love that, irrespective of whether I am riding in Sydney's Blue Mountains, Rajasthan India, The Rockies in Canada or the Dolomites in Italy, local motorcyclists will join alongside and share the best experiences of their country with me. The exhilaration of competing or simply riding through small country towns along roads with stunning scenery and in all weather, creates lasting memories and friendships that brings so much joy and shared happiness. I only wish I had had female mentors to encourage me along as a junior.*

Until she was nine years old Tania lived in Perth. *"I have very fond memories of running out each afternoon to greet my dad arriving home on his work issued Honda 250 motorbike (he was a 'grey ghost' parking inspector). First dad would have me guess what he had for me in the bike pannier – and I was always lucky to find it being an 'ice-cream sandwich' or a 'Hazelnut Roll'. He would then lift me up onto the back of the bike and take me for a dinky around the block. There I would sit, proud as punch, enjoying the wind in my hair, ice-cream melting all over me and the biggest smile on face. Those dinkies around the block set me up for a lifetime of love for motorbikes (and ice-cream)."*

In the early 1980s, Tania's family made what they described as *"the best decision"* to move to York, a small farming community just 100 km from Perth. *"We rarely ventured back to the city and I didn't mind at all. My childhood was idyllic, with my days spent exploring the countryside on horseback and on my pushbike. I loved being out in the open, clean air and being able to roam free from dawn to dusk."*

Comfortable in her own skin aboard a motorcycle.

In one respect though, Tania was a bit of a 'square peg in a round hole' In an Australian country town, male and female roles were firmly defined. Although Tania was fascinated by motorcycles, riding just wasn't an activity that girls were encouraged to do! One fine day, Tania's curiosity got the better of her when she boldly ventured down to the local motocross track. "*One of the boys offered to take me on the back. Thirty years later, and I still have the scar on my shin after going airborne and landing on the serrated foot peg. I also had an occasion where some boys thought it would be hilarious to chase me on their dirt-bikes through the bush. At the time, I was out training for a cross country run. In pure fright, I found a surge of energy and sprinted up a hill behind Mount Brown. Although the experience was stressful it set me up well for the race and I was able to outpace and win on the final hill climb.*"

When Tania turned 15 and after much begging, her Dad agreed to buy her her own motorbike. It was a Honda – a model not dissimilar to what he was familiar with from his days as a parking inspector. Not ideal for a first bike, especially as the only place that she could ride it was around the fire break around a paddock. "*Regardless, I was out after school doing laps through the boggy soil. As I rode down our long sandy driveway to return home, I had a flashback to the thrill of riding as a pillion with dad and wanted to open the throttle. And I did. Before I knew it, I was just metres from the garage and with really no idea on how to brake correctly. At that moment, my mum came outside and witnessed me crash the bike and slide into the garage. An hour later, everything was gaffer taped together, and dad and I were riding it back to Perth where it was sold. I was gutted as I knew it would be many years before I would have a chance to ride again.*"

Alongside husband Nenad gracing the roads on Royal Enfields.

In her early 20s, and after travelling to India and Japan inspired by the number of motorbikes around her. Tania returned to Perth and got her much dreamed of motorcycle licence - albeit one restricted to learner-approved motorcycles only. Tania envisaged her motorcycling journey to include the thrill and complexity of road racing! The race track beckoned Tania but she found that whenever she mentioned it to her friends, she was met with a barrage of discouraging comments, *"Girls don't race, it's too hard, you are not aggressive enough, it's too expensive and you don't have a suitable bike!"*

Enjoying a Trail and Enduro Rally.

When Tania turned 26 she decided to up the ante and get her open class licence and a 'big' bike. She set her sights on a Honda CBR600, which was then considered a sport bike that could stay with anything else on the road.

She decided to do it right this time and get professional riding tuition rather than be taught by nay-saying motorcycling friends. After a quick study of the relevant section of the Perth Yellow Pages, Tania arranged a lesson with a school Advantage Motorcycle Rider Training. She met and instantly gelled with Nenad Djurdjevic, the owner/operator of the school. Nenad became Tania's coach and mentor and inspired Tania further along her motorcycling path sharing not only his passion for riding in all its forms (sport, touring dirt, adventure), but also for motorcycle safety and motorcyclists' rights. Nenad recalls: *"I first met Tania when she was 26 when she booked a lesson with my motorcycle rider training school to prepare for her open class licence test. She originally was due to have her first lesson with another instructor but had to change her appointment so that I took her lesson. The rest as they say is history, and we have been together ever since!"* Nenad not only encouraged her to get her race licence, but followed up by working through the night to prep her race bikes and was there as Tania's moral support and pit crew. *"From the very first lesson, I knew I had finally met someone who understood my passion and shared it 100%. This was not a guy who just liked the idea of owning a bike, or going for a lap around the city streets of Perth on a Wednesday night. He wanted to explore the world on the back of a bike. We were married two years later and have together ridden around the incredible Dolomites of Italy, the passes of Austria, the mountains in New Zealand, Vietnam and bare roads of India. We have explored our own backyard on road and dirt, and ridden every squiggly line we could find in Tasmania and in the Adelaide Hills. In the process, we have built up an amazing band of friends that have joined us along the way."*

Nenad removed the barriers that Tania felt stopped her from discovering motorcycling earlier in life!

"After getting her open licence in short order, it wasn't long before the student exceeded her instructor" Nenad explained. *"She was a natural rider who, while knowing little about the technical aspects of her machine, had that elusive 'feel' that makes for a successful racer. I remember trying to catch and overtake her on a winding road to tell her she had missed a turnoff and realised I had my task cut out for me when I hit the rev cut out on my 750 with the tacho needle buried well into the red zone! Suffice to say I decided to get a faster bike after that! But nothing has changed, whether on the open road, racetrack or a forest trail on dirt bikes; whenever Tania is ahead of me on a motorcycle and gets into her stride, like Jorge Lorenzo on a good day, the gap just widens until she disappears into the distance. I can only imagine how good a rider she would have been if she had started riding earlier and was brought up in a culture where women motorcyclists were common rather than unusual."*

Tania is now in the position to have a bit of time on the weekends to enjoy and revel in the freedom of recreational riding alongside her husband on the open roads of Australia and, no doubt, the world.

"My goal now is to create opportunities for all children to get involved with the sport and break down the entry barriers to participate. Although I don't race anymore, I still practice on the track at Philip Island and Eastern Creek. I also enter Trail and Enduro events and work to keep up different skills - the next I am learning is Trials and how to do a wheelie at the Wheelie school."

"Hopefully the next generation of girls will be inspired by her and other pioneering women riders and the gap in participation and performance between male and female motorcyclists will be closed."
Nenad Djurdjevic

Photos supplied by Tania Lawrence

APPENDIX

AUSTRALIAN GROUPS THAT SUPPORT AND ENCOURAGE WOMEN MOTORCYCLISTS

MOTORCYCLING VICTORIA - PARTICIPATION

Motorcycling Victoria is taking proactive steps forward to increase and promote female participation in motorcycling sport across the state as Riders, Officials, Coaches and Volunteers.

The Female Participation Program endeavours to change perceptions around the roles of females within the sport and to bring about sustainable cultural change to support females in all areas of the sport now and for the future.

Investing in a full-time staff member, Peta Thomas, to manage the Female Participation Program, it has given MV the resources to work towards implementing a long-term change in regards to the perceptions around the roles of females within the sport and bringing about a sustainable cultural change to support female participation in all areas now and for the future.

Amongst other events, Participation hosts Girls Only Track Days.

Website: www.motorcyclingvic.com.au

WOMEN'S INTERNATIONAL MOTORCYCLE ASSOCIATION (WIMA)

WIMA is an international organisation that promotes, encourages and supports motorcycling amongst women with members in 22 countries including Australia. Members meet annually in a different country for a rally that welcomes all members and their family. Recent rallies have been in Sweden, Poland, Switzerland and Hungary. Estonia will host the 2017 rally. WIMA is for women who are interested in motorcycling in all its forms, and you don't have to ride or own a bike to be a member. It may be your children's motocross or mini bike activities, an interest in motorcycle racing, or even the daily commute on your scooter. Our organisation has been active in Australia since 1984. We encourage the attendance of the members' male family and friends, and they are most welcome at rides, rallies and events.

Contact us at: wima.org.au or wimaaus@gmail.com

LADIES OF HARLEY (LOH)

The Harley Owners Group® (H.O.G.®) is the world's largest manufacturer-sponsored motorcycle club that has approximately 1 million members worldwide. It began in 1983 as a way to create a strong bond between the motor company and riders and has developed into a dynamic brother and sisterhood of likeminded riders all celebrating, enjoying and creating the Harley-Davidson lifestyle.

As more and more women chose to ride, a way was sought to encourage women to become more active members of H.O.G. and their local chapters as both riders and passengers, so Ladies of Harley (LOH) was born.

LOH is not a separate organization to H.O.G. Chapters but is a group within the chapter. There is no charge to join LOH but being part of LOH is not automatic, as women must elect to become part of it in their H.O.G. renewal process. One of the benefits of being a full, life or associate H.O.G. member, is the opportunity to join LOH within a chapter.

Each renewal year, LOH members receive a pin and can purchase patches.

Many women love being part of LOH as Nola and Hana testify

"Since being involved with LOH I have met many great friends with the same enthusiasm and passion for riding a Harley Davidson. Whether we do a day ride, an overnighter, long road trips or other activities, it's about getting together and sharing our passion. We welcome and encourage new riders in joining and look out for each other. LOH is like family."

Nola Watson

"At the age of 45 I secured my full motorbike licence and at the same time purchased my first Harley. I didn't know any other Harley Riders so I thought it would be a great idea to join the Sydney HOG Chapter, best decision I have made. This Chapter and riding my bike was my saving grace. The best thing is that we have fun, we have yummy coffee/food and we are able to build great relationships. Participating in LOH has allowed me to ride confidently with big groups, we share tips that help one another and we acknowledge our women pillion riders and those who eventually transition onto their own bikes."

Hana Grant
Website: https://members.hog.com, **Tel:** 1 800 HOGCLUB (464 258)

KYSA MOTORBIKES

Kysa Moto Bikes is a unique ladies motorcycle group that caters for all women riders from beginners to advanced, any style or type of motorbike and women of any age! Founder, Kylie Sage, started riding when she was 10 years of age, then in 2010 she realized the need for female companionship whilst riding and so she created Kysa. Kysa Ladies Motorcycle Group is all about riding – laughing – eating – friends – fun – learning – supporting each other – fund raising for needy and worthwhile projects (like the Black Dog Ride) and getting out on the bike and exploring some fantastic roads with other like-minded people!

Email: kylie@kysa.com.au
Website: www.kysa.com.au

GIRLS RIDE OUT

Girls Ride Out was formed in April 2001 by Selena Thurbon, from a need to ride with other women. In 2004 they became incorporated and remain a social group of mostly women, who stay in touch through e-mail, Facebook and of course regular rides. GRO schedules monthly rides for all 3 chapters, organise charity events, operate a support network for learner riders and conduct the occasional maintenance day. Girls Ride Out also has an active Facebook group and a website for hints, tips, organising impromptu rides, and more. Most members are in Sydney but there is also a chapter in Newcastle and on the Central Coast of NSW. The Pink Ribbon Motorcycle Ride in Sydney is organised by GRO and attracts well over 1000 riders to the event & raising over $50,000 every year for Breast Cancer.

Website: www.girlsrideout.com

Facebook: GirlsRideOut

WOMEN 2 WHEELS (MOTORCYCLE NETWORK SA)

In the year of 2012, two women met by chance through a social event and discovered they had a mutual interest in motorcycling. Toni Barwick and Mary Knights formed a friendship which grew from simple outings together riding their bikes, to figuring out how they could connect with other women riders living in Adelaide, South Australia. Facebook was the medium of choice so they formed the group *Women 2 Wheels* (W2W) in March 2013. As time went by, the Facebook page gained momentum as women heard about it through word of mouth. Inspired by the growing interest and participation, Toni and Mary began to run events, starting with day rides through to weekend trips. The women continued to join the group and this allowed for major events to be coordinated. For two women with no funds behind them, they managed to get a women's only track day happening at the Mallala motorsports circuit; build up annual events such as the official rides for the International Female Ride Day and Pink Ribbon Rides and continue to support other motorcycling club's charity events. *Women 2 Wheels* is now a recognised name in Adelaide that has built a good reputation as a supportive network for women motorcyclists. Members are as diverse in their motorcycling interest as the types of motorcycles they own and ride.

Facebook: Women 2 Wheels (Motorcycle Network SA)